Life Is Not Hard

A New Blueprint for Living with Ease, Meaning, and Freedom

By
**Mardoche Sidor, MD
Karen Dubin, PhD, LCSW
And the SWEET Institute**

SWEET Institute Publishing
Transformational Books for a Transformational World

Copyright © 2025 by the SWEET Institute

All rights reserved. No part of this book may be reproduced, stored in a retrieval system, or transmitted in any form or by any means—electronic, mechanical, photocopying, recording, or otherwise—without the prior written permission of the publisher, except in the case of brief quotations embodied in critical articles or reviews.

Published by:
SWEET Institute Publishing
New York, NY
WWW.SWEETInstitutePublishing.com

First Edition
Printed in the United States of America

ISBN (Paperback): 978-1-968105-14-3
Library of Congress Control Number: [pending]

Cover Design by SWEET Institute Publishing

Interior Design and Layout by SWEET Institute Publishing

For bulk orders, permissions, or media inquiries, please contact:
sweetinstitutepublishing@sweetinstitute.com

Unless otherwise noted, all stories and case examples in this book are either fictionalized or used with permission, and identifying details have been changed to protect the privacy of individuals.

SWEET Institute Publishing
Transformational Books for a Transformational World

Dedication

To all those who have been told that life must be a struggle.

May these pages remind you that ease, joy, and grace are your birthright.

To every seeker who has walked through hardship —not because you had to, but because you were strong enough to rise from it —this book is for you.

And to our families, our communities, and the people we serve,
who teach us daily that transformation is possible:
we dedicate this work with love and gratitude.

Also by the Authors

Mardoche Sidor, M.D.; Karen Dubin, Ph.D., LCSW; with the SWEET Institute

- Journey to Empowerment
- Discovering Your Worth: Everything You Need to Feel Fulfilled
- The Power of Faith: A Harvard-Trained Psychiatrist Speaking on Faith
- The Psychotherapy Certificate Course: The Clinician and Coach Manual (Books 1–3)
- The Anxiety Course: The Workbook
- What's Missing
- NLP for Clinicians
- 50 SWEET Poems: Reflections on Life, Love, and Self
- The Power of Belief: How Ideas Shape Leaders, Nations, and the Future
- The Courage to Care: Stories of Healing, Hope, and the Power of Social Work — Told by Over 50 SWEET Institute Social Workers
- Transforming Team Relationships from the Inside Out: The SWEET Healing Circle for Agencies — Redefining Accountability, Collaboration, and Culture
- Remembering: The Journey Back to the Pre-Conditioned Self
- The Clinician's Mirror: A Story of Projection, Self-Awareness, and Transformation for Clinicians
- The Secret Is in Remembering: Why We Suffer, Why We Forget, and How to Return to Who We Are
- It's All Perfect: What If Nothing in Your Life Was a Mistake?
- Because of Us: Why Outcomes Change When We Do

- Before Anything Else, Validate: The Missing Link in Healing, Leadership, Relationships, and Personal Growth
- Rewriting the Script: The Power of Transforming Inner Dialogue in Oppressed Communities
- Determined to See: A Science-Based and Story-Driven Integration of A Course in Miracles and the Four Layers of Transformation
- Always Enough: The Transformational Power of Unconditional Positive Regard
- How to See, Accept, and Elevate Yourself and Others Through the 4 Layers of Transformation
- Becoming the Very Best

Table of Contents

Foreword by Doreen Plante, LCSW-R, BCD — 11
Preface by Jeanne Weiner, LCSW — 13
Introduction — 15
    Why This Book? — 17
    What This Book Is About — 19
    How to Read This Book — 20
    How This Book Works — 21
Front Acknowledgments — 23
Prologue — 24
Part I: Rethinking Life's Hardness — 25
    Chapter 1: The Weight We Carry — 26
    Chapter 2: The University of Struggle — 30
    Chapter 3: An Alternative Classroom — 34
Part II: The Four Layers of Transformation — 38
    Chapter 4: Layer One – Conscious Transformation — 40
    Chapter 5: Layer Two – Preconscious Transformation — 43
    Chapter 6: Layer Three – Unconscious Transformation — 47
    Chapter 7: Layer Four – Existential Transformation — 51
Part III: From Effort to Integration — 55
    Chapter 8: The Spiral of Growth — 56
    Chapter 9: Life as Lightness — 59
    Chapter 10: The Still Point — 63
    Chapter 11: Everyday Integration – Living the Four Layers — 67
    Chapter 12: From Effort to Embodiment — 71

Chapter 13: The Dance of Wholeness 75

Chapter 14: Habits of Ease – Structuring a Life That Flows 79

Chapter 15: Resilience Without Struggle 83

Chapter 16: Love Without Hardness 86

Chapter 17: Parenting with Lightness 90

Chapter 18: Friendship, Belonging, and Joy 93

Chapter 19: Work and Service as Play 96

Chapter 20: Collective Transformation – Building Communities of Ease 99

Part IV: The Barriers to Ease **102**

Chapter 21: Why We Cling to Hardness 103

Chapter 22: The Hidden Comfort of Struggle 106

Chapter 23: Defenses Against Lightness 109

Chapter 24: Meeting Fear with Presence 112

Chapter 25: Beyond Trauma – Healing at All Four Layers 115

Part V: The Existential Turn **118**

Chapter 26: Choosing Freedom, Choosing Responsibility 119

Chapter 27: The Compass of Values 123

Chapter 28: The Golden Rule Reimagined 126

Chapter 29: The Existential Leap – Saying Yes to Life 129

Chapter 30: Life as Grace 133

Conclusion **136**

Epilogue **137**

Invitation to the Reader **138**

Final Acknowledgments **139**

Reader Integration Toolkit **140**

Appendix	**142**
Recommended Reading	**150**
More from SWEET Institute Publishing	**152**
About the Authors	**153**

Foreword

by Doreen Plante, LCSW-R, BCD

When I was first invited to write the foreword for *Life is Not Hard*, I paused. The very title challenges one of the deepest cultural assumptions we carry, which is that life is meant to be endured, not enjoyed; and fought through, not flowed with. As a clinician who has sat with countless individuals navigating suffering, I have witnessed how deeply the myth of hardship shapes our identity, relationships, and even our sense of worth.

What struck me most as I read this manuscript is that it does not deny suffering. Instead, it offers a radical yet profoundly humane reframe: hardship is not a requirement for growth. Struggle may shape us, but it does not define us. Healing, learning, and transformation are not dependent on pain; rather, they can emerge from love, presence, joy, and grace.

The SWEET Institute brings together science, clinical wisdom, and lived experience in a way that is both rigorous and deeply compassionate. Their four-layer model — conscious, preconscious, unconscious, and existential — offers a roadmap that is as practical as it is profound. This book moves beyond intellectual understanding, inviting us into embodiment, practice, and integration.

What I found especially moving are the stories woven throughout — of patients, families, communities, and the authors themselves. These stories remind us that the path of transformation is not abstract; rather, it is lived in the everyday moments: in the way we breathe, connect, reflect, and choose.

For clinicians, this book offers tools, frameworks, and insights that will enrich practice. For seekers of growth, it provides clarity, encouragement, and guidance; and for all of us, it offers a gift: the reminder that life, at its core, does not have to be defined by hardship. It can be lived with lightness, resilience, and grace.

It is my hope that as you turn these pages, you allow yourself to consider, deeply and honestly, what it would mean to live from this truth. May you be inspired, challenged, and comforted; and may you walk away with not only new insights, but also the courage to live with greater ease, joy, and presence.

With admiration and gratitude,

Doreen Plante, LCSW-R, BCD
Clinical Social Work/Therapist

Preface

by Jeanne Weiner, LCSW

When I first encountered the work of the SWEET Institute, I was struck by their unwavering commitment to one essential truth: change is possible, and it does not have to come through suffering alone. As a clinician, I have seen how many people believe that growth must be earned through hardship, and that resilience only counts when it is forged in fire. But the pages you hold in your hands tell a different story, and one that is both scientifically grounded and deeply human.

This book does not deny the reality of suffering; rather, it reframes it, as life will present us with challenges, but we are not defined by how much we endure. We are defined by how we learn, integrate, and transform. The brilliance of this work lies in its model — the four layers of transformation: conscious, preconscious, unconscious, and existential. Each layer illuminates a new dimension of change, moving us from behavior to belief, from memory to meaning, from effort to grace.

What makes this book unique is its balance. It is rigorous yet accessible, filled with science yet alive with story. It offers tools and practices that are immediately usable, while also challenging us to think more deeply about the lives we are creating. It respects both the intellect and the spirit; and for clinicians, it is a resource, for seekers, it is a guide, and for all of us, it is an invitation.

Reading these chapters, I was reminded of my own work with clients who long for relief, for lightness, for a way to live that is not bound by the myth of hardship. Time and again, I have witnessed the transformation that comes when someone realizes: 'I am not my struggle. I am more. I am free to choose another way.' This book captures that realization and gives it shape, language, and practice.

As you turn these pages, I encourage you not only to read, but to reflect, to pause, to apply. The authors remind us that information is not enough, and that it ought to become lived experience. May this book inspire you to embrace ease without guilt, growth without punishment, and life as the gift it already is.

With gratitude for the journey,
Jeanne Weiner, LCSW

Introduction

by Mardoche Sidor, MD, and Karen Dubin, PhD, LCSW

We wrote this book because of a question we heard again and again, both in our work as clinicians and in our own lives: Does life have to be this hard?

In our offices, in hospitals, in community settings, and in conversations with friends and family, we encountered the same belief, that struggle is inevitable, and perhaps even necessary, for growth. This belief is deeply woven into our culture. We glorify endurance, elevate sacrifice, and define resilience only in terms of what has been survived. And yet, what if this belief itself is what keeps us bound? What if growth, healing, and transformation do not require suffering as their fuel?

This book is our attempt to answer that question. It is grounded in science, informed by decades of clinical practice, and enriched by our collaboration with the SWEET Institute community. Here, we explore a simple but radical premise: life does not have to be hard. Hard things will happen, but hardship is not the measure of our worth, for growth does not need to be earned in pain, and meaning does not require struggle as its gatekeeper.

To make this journey clear, we introduce the Four Layers of Transformation — conscious, preconscious, unconscious, and existential. These layers represent the full arc of change:

- At the conscious level, we shift behaviors, routines, and habits.
- At the preconscious level, we uncover patterns and beliefs that shape how we see ourselves and others.
- At the unconscious level, we bring repressed material into awareness and learn to work through it.
- At the existential level, we choose meaning, responsibility, and freedom, integrating all that has come before.

Together, these four layers provide a map, and not only for healing but also for living. This model reflects the truth we have seen in countless lives: change is not just possible; rather, it is sustainable, when it moves through all these layers.

This book is both theoretical and practical. It offers stories, research, tools, and reflections to help you not just understand, but also practice. Our goal is to move beyond intellectual insight into embodied change; and ach chapter invites you to pause, reflect, and apply, for knowledge alone does not transform; rather, practice does.

We wrote this book not as distant experts, but as fellow travelers. We, too, have known struggle. We, too, have had to learn that life can be lived with more lightness, grace, and joy. This is a message we believe the world needs urgently: that ease is not weakness, that joy is not naïve, and that grace is not accidental; rather, they are choices, orientations, and practices available to all of us.

As you read, we invite you to suspend the old assumption that life must be hard; and we invite you to experiment with a new perspective: what if life could be different? What if lightness is not the exception, but the truth we had forgotten?

Welcome to your new life.

With warmth and gratitude,

Mardoche Sidor, MD
Karen Dubin, PhD, LCSW

Why This Book?

Because we live in a world that glorifies struggle, rewards overwork, celebrates exhaustion, and equates worth with endurance. Somewhere along the way, we began to believe that life must be difficult to be meaningful; yet what if this is not true? What if hardship is not the prerequisite for growth, but merely one of many paths through which growth can occur?

This book was born from countless conversations with patients, colleagues, and community members who asked: Why does life have to be so hard? Our answer, which is the premise of this book, is simple but transformative: it doesn't. Life will bring challenges, but we do not need to make suffering the measure of our existence.

The timing for this book could not be more urgent. Across the globe, people are facing burnout, anxiety, depression, disconnection, and the weight of relentless demands. Clinicians are stretched thin, families are fractured by stress, and communities are searching for hope. Old models that center struggle as the only gateway to resilience are no longer enough. We need a new framework; one that honors suffering without glorifying it, and that opens pathways to ease, joy, and integration.

This is why we offer the Four Layers of Transformation: conscious, preconscious, unconscious, and existential. This model bridges science and lived experience, therapy and philosophy, research and practice. It provides a practical map for change that does not stop at insight but carries us through to embodied transformation.

This book matters because the world needs a new narrative. We need to remember that life can be lived with lightness, that healing can arise from presence and connection, and that grace is not an exception but an ever-present possibility.

We wrote this book for clinicians who long for tools that go deeper, for seekers who crave meaning without martyrdom, and for anyone who has ever whispered to themselves in the quiet of night: Does it really have to be this hard?

Our answer is no; and this book is our invitation to discover another way.

What This Book Is About

This book is about remembering a truth that has been hidden beneath layers of cultural conditioning: life does not have to be hard.

Yes, challenges will come; and yes, pain is part of the human experience; but suffering is not the currency of growth, nor the sole teacher of meaning. Too often we glorify hardship, believing it is the only path to resilience or wisdom; yet his book offers another way, a way grounded in science, shaped by clinical practice, and illuminated by human experience.

At its heart, this book introduces the Four Layers of Transformation:

1. The Conscious Layer – where we shape our habits, routines, and choices, building the structures of daily life.
2. The Preconscious Layer – where we uncover the patterns, schemas, and beliefs that quietly guide us.
3. The Unconscious Layer – where hidden memories, defenses, and repressed material rise into awareness to be worked through.
4. The Existential Layer – where we integrate everything into freedom, purpose, and meaning, choosing how we want to live.

Through these four layers, transformation becomes whole. The book guides you step by step — from conscious action to deep reflection, from hidden wounds to existential freedom. Along the way, you will encounter tools, reflections, practices, and scientific insights that bridge knowledge and embodiment.

This is not only a book to read, but a book to live. Each chapter blends narrative, science, and practice, inviting you to experiment, to pause, to apply. It is written for clinicians, seekers, and anyone who has ever wondered if life could be lighter, more joyful, and more whole.

This book is about reclaiming life as gift, and not defined by hardship, but enriched by presence, connection, and grace.

How to Read This Book

This book is not meant to be rushed. It is not a manual to skim or a checklist to complete. It is an invitation to slow down, to reflect, and to integrate.

Each chapter is built with three elements:

- Narrative — stories that illuminate the themes and bring them to life.
- Science — research and frameworks that ground the message in evidence.
- Practice — tools, reflections, and prompts to help you embody the ideas.

You may choose to read from start to finish, allowing the book's sequence to guide you step by step through the Four Layers of Transformation: conscious, preconscious, unconscious, and existential. Or you may choose to open to the chapter that calls to you in the moment, trusting that you will find what you need.

What matters most is not how much you read, but how deeply you apply. Transformation does not come from knowing more, but from living differently. We encourage you to:

- Pause often.
- Reflect on the questions.
- Try the practices.
- Journal about what arises.
- Return to chapters again and again as you grow.

This book is not only for the mind. It is for the body, the heart, and the spirit. Approach it not as a textbook, but as a companion. Carry it with you into your daily life, into your breath, your relationships, and your choices.

If you do, you will discover that these are not just words on a page; rather, they are a path, and one that leads from struggle to lightness, from effort to integration, and from hardness to grace.

How This Book Works

This book is designed not just to be read, but to be lived. Each chapter is structured to move you from information to transformation, and from ideas in the mind to practices embodied in daily life.

Here's how it works:

1. Narrative and Storytelling

Each chapter begins with a story — a glimpse into real struggles and real moments of discovery. Stories allow us to connect not just intellectually but emotionally, reminding us that transformation is always human and personal.

2. Conversation

You will often hear our voices in dialogue. These conversations between us as co-authors are designed to model curiosity, questioning, and reflection — the very process we hope you will take into your own life.

3. Science and Theory

Each theme is grounded in evidence — psychology, neuroscience, philosophy, and clinical practice. We provide references so you can see how these ideas stand on both science and lived wisdom.

4. Tools and Practices

Practical exercises, prompts, and reflections are built into every chapter. These are your invitations to experiment, to apply, and to embody what you've read.

5. The Four Layers of Transformation

Every chapter connects back to the framework of conscious, preconscious, unconscious, and existential layers. This ensures that learning is not one-dimensional but integrated across all levels of being.

6. Integration and Reflection

Each chapter closes with reflection questions to help you pause, digest, and weave the material into your daily life.

This book is not linear in the sense that you must follow every step in sequence. You can start at the beginning and move forward, or you can open to the chapter that speaks to your current need. What matters most is that you practice.

The more you bring these ideas into your routines, your beliefs, your hidden narratives, and your existential choices, the more you will discover: life does not have to be hard. It can be lived with lightness, integration, and grace.

Front Acknowledgments

This book could not have come into being without the countless people who shaped, supported, and inspired its creation.

First, to the individuals, families, and communities who entrusted us with your stories: You are our greatest teachers. Your courage, resilience, and humanity breathe life into every page of this book.

To our communities at the SWEET Institute and Urban Pathways, thank you for your partnership, your dedication, and your vision. Together, we continue to explore what it means to transform lives not through struggle, but through presence, connection, and grace.

To our mentors and teachers, those who guided us in medicine, social work, psychology, psychoanalysis, philosophy, spirituality, and beyond: We are indebted to your wisdom. You showed us that science and humanity need not be separated, but can enrich one another.

To our families, who remind us daily that love is the foundation of all transformation. Thank you for your patience, your encouragement, and your unwavering belief in this work.

And to every reader who chooses to pick up this book, thank you. By opening these pages, you have already begun the process. You are the reason we wrote this, and you are the hope that these ideas will live beyond us.

With deep gratitude,

Mardoche Sidor, MD
Karen Dubin, PhD, LCSW

Prologue

There is a moment, often quiet, when the question arises: Does it really have to be this hard?

It may come late at night, when the house is still. It may come in the middle of a busy day, hidden beneath exhaustion. It may come after loss, heartbreak, or simply another overwhelming to-do list. In that moment, we glimpse a truth we often ignore: perhaps life was never meant to be lived as a constant uphill battle.

We have been taught otherwise. Our culture has conditioned us to believe that worth comes from struggle, that meaning must be carved out of pain, that resilience is proven only in suffering. These messages are so deeply ingrained that they feel like truth. What if they are not?

This book begins with a radical proposition: life does not have to be hard. Hard things will happen, struggle is part of the human story; yet hardship is not the measure of our worth, nor the only path to growth, for there are other ways, ways rooted in presence, in connection, and in grace.

The chapters ahead will take you on a process through the Four Layers of Transformation — conscious, preconscious, unconscious, and existential. You will see how each layer holds keys not only to healing but to living differently. This is not a denial of suffering, but a reframe of its place in our lives.

The prologue is an invitation, and a reminder that as you turn these pages, you are stepping into a possibility too often forgotten: that life can be lighter, that happiness can be a teacher, and that grace can be the ground we walk upon.

Let this be your beginning.

Part I: Rethinking Life's Hardness

Chapter 1: The Weight We Carry

It was 3 a.m., and Daniel lay awake staring at the ceiling. The day had been heavy — deadlines missed, arguments with his partner, and the feeling that no matter how much he tried, life always found a way to push him down. The thought looped in his mind like a broken record: *'Life is hard. It's always been hard. And it will always be hard.'*

Daniel didn't realize that this belief wasn't just a passing thought; rather, it was a story he had carried since childhood. His parents, having grown up in scarcity, often repeated, 'Nothing comes easy in this life.' At school, teachers emphasized discipline through struggle. In church, sermons highlighted suffering as the price of virtue. By the time Daniel was an adult, the weight of this story had fused with his identity. He didn't just believe life was hard; rather, he believed *he was meant to live a hard life.*

But was it true? Was life really meant to be hard — or was it simply a narrative passed down, reinforced by culture, history, and survival instincts? This question would become the starting point for a journey of unlearning and rediscovery.

A Conversation

Mardoche: *Many people carry this invisible backpack of beliefs — 'life is hard,' 'love is painful,' 'success requires suffering.' These are inherited stories, passed on through families and societies, often without question.*

Karen: *Exactly. It's important to differentiate between life containing challenges and life being defined as hard. Challenges are inevitable: illness, loss, change. However, the belief that life itself must be hard is optional. It's a lens we've been taught to look through.*

Mardoche: *Neuroscience tells us that our brains evolved to prioritize survival over happiness. That's why we have what we call in Psychology, the 'negativity bias,' which means we pay more attention to threats than to opportunities (Baumeister et al., 2001). From an evolutionary perspective, it was safer to assume that the rustling in the grass was a predator than to stop and admire the scenery.*

Karen: *The problem is that this bias still operates even when there's no predator. Our minds turn everyday stressors into threats, making life feel harder than it needs to. The good news is, we can train our attention differently, and we can consciously cultivate moments of ease, joy, and presence.*

The Science of Hardness

Science has long studied why humans experience life as difficult. The negativity bias makes negative experiences feel stronger and more memorable than positive ones. This means a single criticism can outweigh five compliments, or one failure can overshadow multiple successes. Baumeister and colleagues (2001) demonstrated that negative events exert a greater impact on our thoughts, emotions, and behaviors than positive ones.

Additionally, cognitive psychology shows that humans engage in 'cognitive fusion,' which is the tendency to merge with our thoughts as if they were literal truths (Hayes et al., 1999). For instance, if the thought 'I am failing' arises, it feels like a fact rather than a passing mental event. When fused with thoughts like 'life is hard,' we experience them not as opinions but as realities.

On the other hand, research in positive psychology reveals that cultivating positive emotions broadens our thinking and builds psychological resources (Fredrickson, 2001). This 'broaden-and-build' theory suggests that joy, love, and gratitude expand awareness and resilience, helping us meet life's challenges with more flexibility.

In short: while our biology primes us for struggle, our psychology equips us with tools to experience more ease.

Tools for Reflection and Practice

1. **Awareness Journal**: For one week, notice every time you think or say, 'Life is hard.' Record the situation, your emotional state, and how your body felt. This helps uncover when and how the story arises.

2. **Cognitive Defusion Practice**: When the thought 'life is hard' comes up, add the phrase 'I am having the thought that…' before it. For example: 'I am having the thought that life is hard.' This simple step creates distance between you and the thought.

3. **Gratitude Pause**: Each night before bed, write down three things that brought ease, joy, or peace. They don't need to be big, and it could be a smile from a stranger, a warm cup of tea, or a deep breath. Over time, this rewires the brain to notice ease as much as struggle.

4. **Body Scan Meditation**: Spend five minutes scanning your body from head to toe. Notice where tension lives. Ask yourself: 'What weight am I carrying today that I can set down?'

Closing Reflection

The weight we carry is not only the challenges of life, but the meaning we attach to them. Life contains difficulties, but it does not have to be lived as a constant burden. We have inherited stories that equate life with struggle, but these stories can be rewritten. By noticing the lens of hardness, questioning its validity, and practicing new ways of seeing, we open the possibility for life to be lighter, more joyful, and more free.

Daniel's sleepless nights were not caused solely by his circumstances, but by the story he carried. As he learned to set down the narrative that 'life is hard,' he began to experience moments of lightness that had always been available to him and waiting beneath the weight.

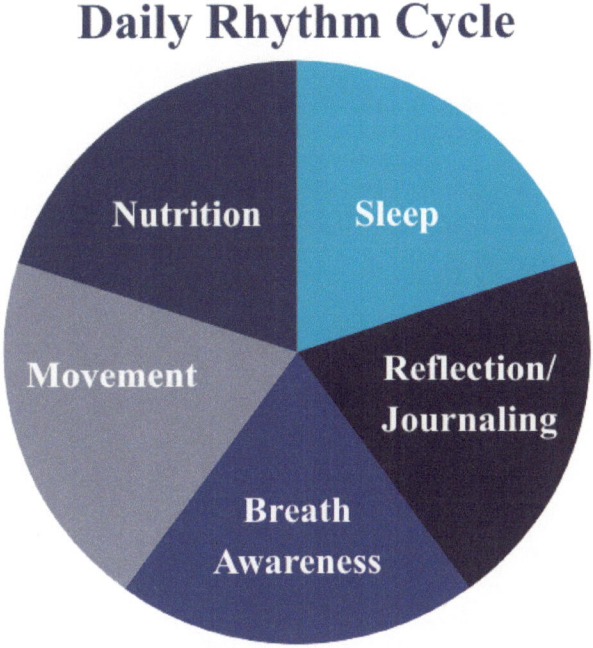

References

- Baumeister, R. F., Bratslavsky, E., Finkenauer, C., & Vohs, K. D. (2001). Bad is stronger than good. Review of General Psychology, 5(4), 323–370.

- Fredrickson, B. L. (2001). The role of positive emotions in positive psychology: The broaden-and-build theory of positive emotions. American Psychologist, 56(3), 218–226.

- Hayes, S. C., Strosahl, K., & Wilson, K. G. (1999). Acceptance and Commitment Therapy: An Experiential Approach to Behavior Change. Guilford Press.

Chapter 2: The University of Struggle

Sophia often said, 'My hardest seasons taught me the most.' She wasn't wrong, and her divorce forced her to discover independence she never thought possible. Her illness reshaped her relationship with her body and taught her to listen more deeply. Her years of financial stress sharpened her creativity and discipline. Each hardship became like a hidden university, and one she never enrolled in but that demanded tuition in the form of tears, sleepless nights, and relentless perseverance.

But as Sophia sat across from her friend one evening, she wondered aloud: 'Did I really need those struggles to learn these lessons? Couldn't I have grown in gentler ways?' This question lingers for many of us: is hardship necessary for growth, or is it simply one of the many teachers life offers?

A Conversation

Karen: *Struggles can be powerful teachers. There's an entire field of research called post-traumatic growth. Tedeschi and Calhoun (2004) found that people who endure hardship often report greater appreciation for life, a deeper sense of spirituality, stronger relationships, and an expanded sense of possibility.*

Mardoche: *That's true, and we need to be careful here. There's a danger in romanticizing suffering. Not everyone who goes through hardship grows from it. Some are crushed, and some never recover. Growth from suffering is not guaranteed, it depends on context, resources, and meaning-making.*

Karen: Exactly. *When people have strong social support, coping strategies, and opportunities to reflect, struggle can become transformative. However, without those supports, hardship can lead to trauma, despair, and cycles of harm.*

Mardoche: *And it's also important to note that joy, curiosity, and love can be equally powerful teachers. A child who grows up in a safe and nurturing environment doesn't need trauma to develop resilience; rather, they build it through exploration, play, and secure relationships.*

The Science of Struggle and Growth

Research on Post-Traumatic Growth (PTG) shows that many individuals report positive psychological changes following adversity. These changes include new perspectives on life, increased resilience, and greater empathy (Tedeschi & Calhoun, 2004). However, PTG is not universal. While some people emerge stronger, others experience lasting psychological scars. Resilience research highlights the role of protective factors, such as supportive relationships, optimism, and effective coping strategies, in determining whether hardship becomes growth or remains as suffering (Masten, 2001).

Developmental psychology also reveals that not all growth requires hardship. Nurturing environments, opportunities for exploration, and moments of joy can foster equally profound transformation. Fredrickson's broaden-and-build theory (2001) demonstrates how positive emotions expand awareness, encourage creativity, and build enduring psychological resources.

In short, struggle can be one teacher among many. It is not the only school available to us, and it is not always the best one.

Tools for Reflection and Practice

1. **Struggle Story Map**: Write about one hardship in your life. Reflect on what it taught you and what it cost you. Ask: Did I need this hardship to learn the lesson or could there have been another way?

2. **Alternative Pathways**: Recall a time when you grew without hardship — perhaps through love, curiosity, or joy. What made that growth possible? What conditions supported it?

3. **Protective Factors Inventory**: List the resources, people, and practices that help you grow today. These protective factors, such as friends, mentors, mindfulness, or creativity, are your 'tuition-free teachers.'

4. **Gratitude for Gentle Teachers**: Each evening, identify one lesson you learned that day without pain or struggle. This retrains your brain to notice the university of joy.

Closing Reflection

Struggles can indeed be teachers. They can strip away illusions, sharpen our sense of meaning, and deepen our compassion. However, they are not prerequisites for growth, for life offers many classrooms: the classroom of hardship, the classroom of curiosity, the classroom of play, and the classroom of love. We do not need to wait for crisis to learn. We can choose to grow daily through the gentle teachers of awareness, connection, and joy.

Sophia realized that while her struggles had shaped her, they were not the only path available. The question she now asked herself was: *'What if I start choosing the classrooms of joy and love more often? What might I learn there?'*

Perhaps the greatest freedom lies not in avoiding hardship, but in recognizing that we are not confined to it as the sole teacher.

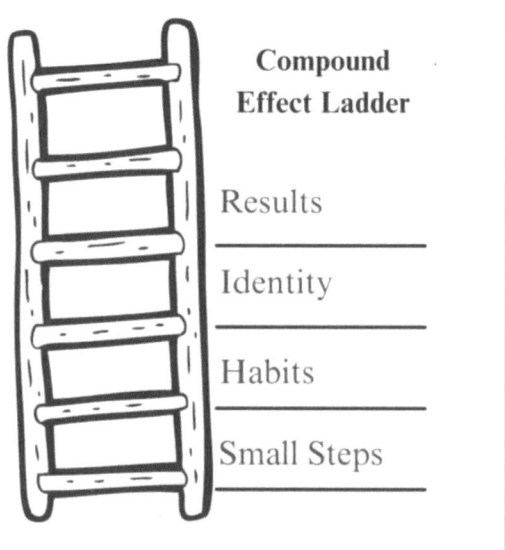

References

- Fredrickson, B. L. (2001). The role of positive emotions in positive psychology: The broaden-and-build theory of positive emotions. American Psychologist, 56(3), 218–226.
- Masten, A. S. (2001). Ordinary magic: Resilience processes in development. American Psychologist, 56(3), 227–238.
- Tedeschi, R. G., & Calhoun, L. G. (2004). Posttraumatic growth: Conceptual foundations and empirical evidence. Psychological Inquiry, 15(1), 1–18.

Chapter 3: An Alternative Classroom

Not all lessons in life need to come through pain. Elias, a musician, discovered this truth in his small studio apartment filled with instruments. For him, growth often arrived through curiosity, exploration, and joy. When he played with sound, layering rhythms, experimenting with melodies, he felt alive, free, and expansive. In those moments of flow, Elias realized he was learning discipline, resilience, and creativity without struggle. He was discovering that life offered another classroom: the classroom of joy, play, and presence.

This chapter explores the possibility that while struggle may sometimes be a teacher, it is not the only one. Growth can come through gentler, more life-affirming pathways. We can expand not only in the storm, but also in the sunlight.

A Conversation

Karen: *Too often, society tells us that only hardship produces growth. However, when we think about children, much of their development comes through play. Play teaches problem-solving, collaboration, and creativity, and reminds us that children don't need trauma to learn these things.*

Mardoche: *Absolutely. In fact, neuroscience shows that play activates the brain's reward systems, strengthens neural connections, builds emotional regulation, and fosters resilience. Animals play, too, and it's an evolutionary tool for growth, not just entertainment.*

Karen: *And joy functions similarly. Barbara Fredrickson's broaden-and-build theory (2001) demonstrates that positive emotions broaden our awareness, encourage exploration, and over time, build enduring resources. In other words, joy is not frivolous; rather, it's transformative.*

Mardoche: *Which means the belief that 'life has to be hard to teach us' is incomplete. Yes, we can learn in hardship; and we can also learn in delight, in curiosity, and in presence. The alternative classroom is available every day, if we're willing to enter it.*

The Science of Joy, Play, and Curiosity

Positive psychology has consistently shown that growth can emerge through positive experiences, not just through adversity. Fredrickson's (2001) broaden-and-build theory explains that positive emotions, like joy, love, and awe, expand our thought-action repertoires, making us more creative, open, and resourceful. Over time, these experiences build lasting psychological and social resources.

Research on play demonstrates its central role in development. Play enhances cognitive flexibility, strengthens social bonds, and improves problem-solving skills (Brown & Vaughan, 2009). Neuroscience studies reveal that play activates the prefrontal cortex, supporting executive function and emotional regulation.

Curiosity, too, drives growth. Kashdan and Silvia (2009) found that curiosity leads people to seek new experiences, tolerate uncertainty, and engage in deeper learning. Far from being a luxury, curiosity is a fundamental driver of psychological resilience and flourishing.

Tools for Reflection and Practice

1. **Flow Journal**: Each day, notice one activity where you felt absorbed and time seemed to disappear. What strengths did you use? What did you learn?
2. **Play Prescription**: Schedule 20 minutes of play this week — whether through a game, art, dance, or unstructured exploration. Reflect on what it taught you about creativity, resilience, or joy.
3. **Curiosity Walk**: Take a 15-minute walk where your only goal is to notice something new, such as a sound, a texture, a small detail you've overlooked before. Journal how this shift in awareness influenced your mood and thinking.

4. **Joy Inventory**: List five activities that consistently bring you joy. These are not distractions; rather, they are doorways to growth. Commit to practicing at least one daily.

Closing Reflection

Hardship may sometimes function as a university, but it is not the only classroom life provides. Joy, play, and curiosity offer equally profound lessons. They expand our minds, strengthen our resilience, and build connections without demanding suffering. The invitation is to recognize that learning and growth can be playful, gentle, and even delightful.

Elias discovered that every time he picked up his guitar, he wasn't just making music; rather, he was entering a classroom of creativity, resilience, and joy. In choosing to learn through lightness, he discovered a truth we can all embrace: *Life is Not Hard* to teach us. Sometimes, its gentlest teachers are the most transformative.

References

- Brown, S., & Vaughan, C. (2009). Play: How it shapes the brain, opens the imagination, and invigorates the soul. Avery.
- Fredrickson, B. L. (2001). The role of positive emotions in positive psychology: The broaden-and-build theory of positive emotions. American Psychologist, 56(3), 218–226.
- Kashdan, T. B., & Silvia, P. J. (2009). Curiosity and interest: The benefits of thriving on novelty and challenge. In S. J. Lopez & C. R. Snyder (Eds.), Oxford Handbook of Positive Psychology (2nd ed., pp. 367–374). Oxford University Press.

Part II: The Four Layers of Transformation

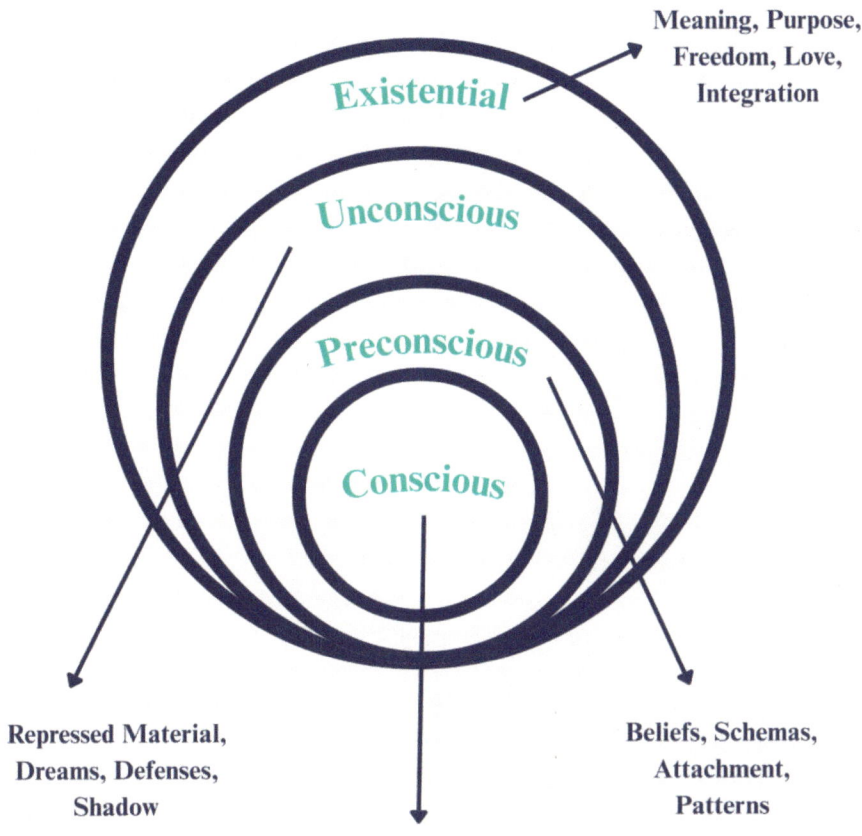

4 Layers Of Transformation Circle

Chapter 4: Layer One – Conscious Transformation

When Mariah decided to take her life back into her own hands, she didn't begin with deep therapy or unraveling old childhood memories. She began with the simplest of steps: going to bed earlier. At first, it seemed almost laughable. Could something as basic as sleep really make a difference? But as the weeks went on, Mariah noticed her mood lifting, her energy increasing, and her ability to handle stress improving. That single act of conscious change began to ripple into her diet, her exercise, her relationships, and eventually, her sense of self. What Mariah was experiencing was the power of transformation at the conscious level.

A Conversation

Karen: *Conscious transformation is about the things we can see, track, and directly influence. It includes our habits, routines, and lifestyle choices. These are the most visible aspects of change.*

Mardoche: *Yes, and it's where most self-help books stop. But that doesn't mean it isn't important. Neuroscience shows that habits literally rewire the brain through neuroplasticity. When people change their sleep, exercise, or nutrition, they're not just shifting behaviors, they're also reshaping neural pathways.*

Karen: *And yet, conscious change requires effort, discipline, and accountability. It's where we often face the challenge of consistency. This is why people relapse on diets, abandon exercise routines, or return to old patterns.*

Mardoche: *Which is why tools like accountability partners, tracking systems, and environmental design matter. We need external supports to make internal changes sustainable.*

The Science of Conscious Change

Behavioral science emphasizes the importance of habit formation. Research by James Clear (2018) and Charles Duhigg (2012) illustrates how habits operate through cues, routines, and rewards. By intentionally reshaping these loops, individuals can build healthier and more productive lives.

Sleep, exercise, and nutrition are particularly powerful levers for conscious transformation. Studies show that adequate sleep improves cognitive function, emotional regulation, and resilience (Walker, 2017). Exercise enhances mood by releasing endorphins and increasing neurogenesis in the hippocampus (Ratey, 2008). Nutrition affects not only physical health but also mental health, with diets rich in whole foods reducing the risk of depression (Jacka et al., 2010).

Mindfulness and meditation also play a key role at the conscious level. Kabat-Zinn (1990) demonstrated that mindfulness-based stress reduction (MBSR) reduces anxiety, improves immune function, and enhances well-being. Conscious practices, though seemingly simple, create the conditions for deeper layers of transformation.

Tools for Reflection and Practice

1. **Habit Tracker**: Choose one small habit (e.g., drinking water in the morning, journaling for 5 minutes, or walking daily). Track it for 30 days, noting how consistency shapes your mood and energy.

2. **Accountability Partner**: Pair with a friend, family member, or colleague. Share your conscious goals weekly and hold each other accountable.

3. **Environmental Design**: Change your environment to make good habits easier and bad habits harder. For example, keep healthy snacks visible and store your phone outside the bedroom.

4. **Stress Reset Practice**: When stress arises, pause for 3 deep breaths. This conscious reset interrupts automatic reactivity and reorients the mind.

5. **Weekly Reflection**: At the end of each week, ask: *'What conscious choices supported me? What choices drained me? What will I carry forward?'*

Closing Reflection

Conscious transformation may look simple — going to bed earlier, eating healthier, breathing deeply. But these practices are not superficial. They are the foundation on which deeper psychological and existential work rests. Mariah's journey reminds us that every act of conscious change is a signal to the self: *'I am worthy of care. I am capable of growth.'* Before we descend into the preconscious and unconscious, we begin here — with the choices that shape our daily lives.

References

- Clear, J. (2018). Atomic Habits: An Easy & Proven Way to Build Good Habits & Break Bad Ones. Avery.
- Duhigg, C. (2012). The Power of Habit: Why We Do What We Do in Life and Business. Random House.
- Jacka, F. N., et al. (2010). Association of Western and traditional diets with depression and anxiety in women. American Journal of Psychiatry, 167(3), 305–311.
- Kabat-Zinn, J. (1990). Full Catastrophe Living: Using the Wisdom of Your Body and Mind to Face Stress, Pain, and Illness. Delacorte.
- Ratey, J. J. (2008). Spark: The Revolutionary New Science of Exercise and the Brain. Little, Brown.
- Walker, M. (2017). Why We Sleep: Unlocking the Power of Sleep and Dreams. Scribner.

Chapter 5: Layer Two – Preconscious Transformation

James always wondered why he kept sabotaging relationships. On the surface, he wanted love and connection. But time and again, as soon as things grew intimate, he withdrew or pushed the other person away. To his frustration, he found himself repeating the same pattern, even when he consciously resolved to act differently. What James didn't yet realize was that the answers lay not in his conscious choices, but in the patterns stored beneath them — in the preconscious layer of his mind, where schemas and core beliefs quietly directed his behavior.

The preconscious layer is where our automatic patterns, learned templates, and emotional blueprints reside. It is the domain of attachment styles, schemas, and internalized beliefs that guide how we perceive the world and ourselves. Unlike the unconscious, which is hidden, the preconscious is accessible, and it is the just-below-the-surface layer. By bringing awareness to these patterns, we can begin to shift them and create new possibilities for living.

A Conversation

Karen: *The preconscious is fascinating because it explains why people can consciously want change but still feel stuck. It's like trying to swim upstream against hidden currents.*

Mardoche: Exactly. *Think of schemas as the mental templates we develop in childhood. If someone grows up with inconsistent care, they may develop a schema of abandonment. So even as an adult, they interpret neutral behaviors, such as a partner being quiet, as rejection.*

Karen: *And this is where therapies like schema therapy, ACT, and Gestalt become so powerful. They help us identify and work with these patterns instead of just fighting them at the surface.*

Mardoche: *Yes, and mindfulness helps us notice when a pattern is operating. When someone realizes, 'Ah, this isn't reality, this is my schema reacting,' they step into choice instead of automatic reaction.*

The Science of Schemas and Patterns

Schemas are deeply ingrained mental frameworks that shape how we interpret experiences. Jeffrey Young's schema theory (Young et al., 2003) identifies maladaptive schemas such as abandonment, mistrust, and defectiveness, which can drive lifelong struggles if unexamined. These schemas are often formed in childhood and carried into adulthood.

Attachment theory further illuminates the preconscious. Bowlby (1969) and Ainsworth (1978) showed how early caregiving relationships establish internal working models of trust, security, and connection. These attachment patterns — secure, anxious, avoidant, or disorganized — become the silent scripts through which adults approach relationships.

Cognitive and acceptance-based therapies highlight the importance of defusion and reappraisal. ACT, for example, teaches individuals to notice thoughts and schemas without fusing with them (Hayes et al., 1999). Gestalt therapy emphasizes awareness of present-moment patterns, allowing people to experiment with new ways of being.

Tools for Reflection and Practice

1. **Schema Journal**: Reflect on recurring themes in your struggles. Do you often feel abandoned, unworthy, or mistrustful? Write down the situations that activate these beliefs.

2. **Pattern Interruption**: When a familiar negative thought or reaction arises, pause and say: *'This is my schema speaking, not reality.'* Then choose a small, different response.

3. **Attachment Map**: Identify your attachment style by reflecting on how you approach closeness, independence, and conflict. Notice how these patterns influence your current relationships.

4. **Compassionate Reparenting**: Imagine what you would say to a child experiencing the same schema-driven fear you feel. Practice speaking to yourself with the same compassion.
5. **Mindfulness of Patterns**: During meditation, bring awareness to recurring thoughts or feelings. Label them as 'schema' or 'pattern,' creating distance from identification.

Closing Reflection

The preconscious layer reveals that much of what we call 'reality' is actually interpretation shaped by old patterns. James's story illustrates how schemas can sabotage even our best intentions, until we bring them into awareness. Transformation at this layer is about noticing, naming, and reshaping the patterns that quietly guide us. When we engage the preconscious with mindfulness, compassion, and therapeutic tools, we loosen the grip of old schemas and open the door to new, freer ways of being.

References

- Ainsworth, M. D. S. (1978). Patterns of Attachment: A Psychological Study of the Strange Situation. Lawrence Erlbaum Associates.
- Bowlby, J. (1969). Attachment and Loss: Vol. 1. Attachment. Basic Books.
- Hayes, S. C., Strosahl, K., & Wilson, K. G. (1999). Acceptance and Commitment Therapy: An Experiential Approach to Behavior Change. Guilford Press.
- Young, J. E., Klosko, J. S., & Weishaar, M. E. (2003). Schema Therapy: A Practitioner's Guide. Guilford Press.

Chapter 6: Layer Three – Unconscious Transformation

Amira always dreamed of becoming a writer, yet every time she sat down to draft a novel, she froze. She blamed procrastination, lack of discipline, or fear of failure. However, underneath these surface explanations, something deeper was at play. In therapy, through free association and dream exploration, Amira uncovered a hidden memory: as a child, she once shared a story she had written, only to be mocked by her teacher and laughed at by classmates. That wound, repressed for decades, had quietly shaped her unconscious belief: *'It isn't safe to create.'*

This is the power of the unconscious layer. It is not simply below awareness; rather, it is guarded, defended, and repressed. Unconscious transformation involves courageously uncovering these hidden forces, bringing them to light, and working through them until they no longer dictate our lives.

A Conversation

Mardoche: *The unconscious is where our defenses, repressed memories, and hidden conflicts live. It influences behavior in ways we don't recognize until we explore it intentionally.*

Karen: *And it's why people can feel stuck even after changing habits and recognizing patterns. They've done the conscious and preconscious work, but the deeper material still holds power.*

Mardoche: *Freud introduced tools like free association, dream analysis, and interpretation precisely for this reason. When people engage with their unconscious material, they discover that their present struggles are often echoes of the past.*

Karen: Exactly. *Defenses like repression, denial, or projection protect us from pain, but they also keep us from freedom. When we gently confront them, we create space for integration.*

Mardoche: *Neuroscience teaches us that implicit memories, which means, our unconscious emotional imprints, influence behavior and physiology even when we have no explicit recollection of the events.*

The Science of the Unconscious

Psychoanalytic theory posits that unconscious processes shape much of human behavior (Freud, 1915). Defenses such as repression, projection, and displacement act as psychological strategies to avoid painful truths. While protective, these mechanisms also create blind spots that perpetuate suffering.

Modern neuroscience validates these ideas. Research on implicit memory shows that experiences encoded without conscious awareness can later influence perception, emotion, and action (Schacter, 1996). Traumatic memories, in particular, are often stored somatically and nonverbally, resurfacing as bodily sensations or triggers (van der Kolk, 2014).

Therapeutic techniques such as free association, dream interpretation, and transference analysis remain powerful pathways for accessing unconscious material. Contemporary methods, including somatic experiencing and EMDR, also target implicit processes to integrate repressed trauma.

Tools for Reflection and Practice

1. **Free Association Journaling**: Set a timer for 10 minutes. Write continuously without censoring or editing. Notice themes or images that emerge, even if they seem unrelated.

2. **Dream Journal**: Record dreams immediately upon waking. Over time, look for recurring symbols or emotions. Reflect on what they might represent about your inner life.

3. **Defense Spotting**: Throughout the week, notice when you feel defensive or reactive. Ask yourself: *'What might I be defending against?'* Write down your reflections.

4. **Working Through**: When you uncover a painful memory or belief, return to it gently over time. Notice how your feelings shift with repeated reflection and support.
5. **Transference Awareness**: Pay attention to how you respond to authority figures, partners, or colleagues. Ask: *'Am I reacting to this person, or to someone from my past they remind me of?'*

Closing Reflection

The unconscious layer is both a storehouse and a protector. It holds not only forgotten memories but also the emotions, conflicts, and longings we once felt were too overwhelming to bear. To engage this layer is to step into the deeper currents of the self, currents that shape our choices without our awareness. Amira's story reminds us that hidden wounds can quietly dictate our lives until they are brought into the light. By uncovering, confronting, and integrating these unconscious forces, we reclaim freedom, creativity, and authenticity.

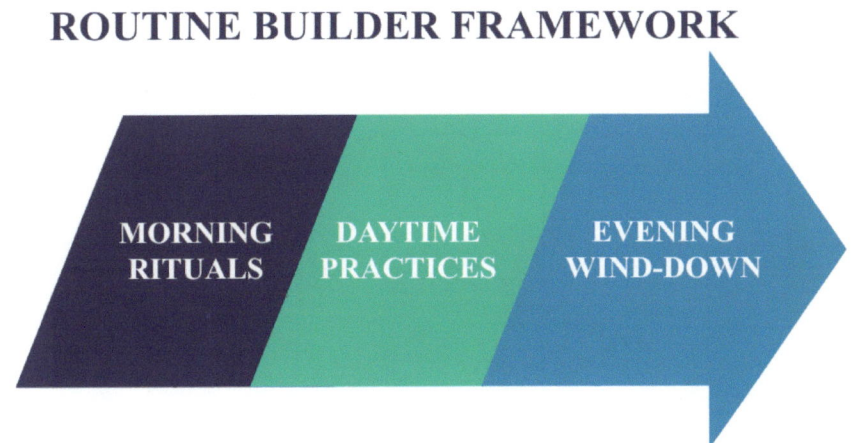

References

- Freud, S. (1915). The unconscious. Standard Edition, 14, 159–215.
- Schacter, D. L. (1996). Searching for Memory: The Brain, the Mind, and the Past. Basic Books.
- van der Kolk, B. A. (2014). The Body Keeps the Score: Brain, Mind, and Body in the Healing of Trauma. Viking.

Chapter 7: Layer Four – Existential Transformation

Diego had spent years working on himself. He had built healthy routines, explored his core beliefs, and even confronted painful memories buried in his unconscious. But something still felt incomplete. One evening, while walking along the beach, he paused to watch the horizon where the ocean met the sky. In that moment of stillness, a question surfaced: *'What is the meaning of my life?'* This was not about habits, schemas, or repressed memories. It was about existence itself, the freedom to choose, the responsibility to create meaning, and the courage to live authentically. Diego had arrived at the existential layer of transformation.

This layer is about integration. It is where the conscious, preconscious, and unconscious converge and open into the broader question of being. Here, we move beyond fixing problems and step into choosing who we want to be. The existential layer is about meaning, freedom, responsibility, and the values that anchor us in life.

A Conversation

Karen: *The existential layer is where people begin to ask the big questions: 'Who am I?' 'Why am I here?' 'What do I want my life to mean?'*

Mardoche: *Exactly. And it's where philosophy meets psychology and neuroscience. Viktor Frankl, in his work on logotherapy, taught that even in the harshest conditions, people can find meaning, and that meaning sustains life (Frankl, 1959).*

Karen: *Existential psychology emphasizes freedom and responsibility. We cannot always control circumstances, but we are free to choose our response, and with that freedom comes the responsibility of shaping our lives.*

Mardoche: *And that choice is guided by values. When people live aligned with their values — compassion, creativity, justice, love — life feels purposeful. Without values, people drift.*

Karen: *The existential layer is also where spiritual and ethical dimensions emerge. The golden rule, for example — 'Do unto others as you would have them do unto you' — becomes not just a moral saying but a compass for authentic living.*

The Science of Meaning and Existence

Existential psychology, developed by thinkers like Viktor Frankl, Rollo May, and Irvin Yalom, emphasizes that humans are meaning-seeking beings. Frankl's logotherapy (1959) demonstrated that finding purpose was central to surviving extreme suffering in concentration camps. Studies show that a sense of meaning is associated with lower rates of depression, higher well-being, and greater resilience (Steger, 2009).

Self-determination theory (Deci & Ryan, 2000) also shows that autonomy, competence, and relatedness are fundamental psychological needs. When these needs are met, individuals report higher motivation and fulfillment.

Existential transformation is not about escaping suffering but integrating it into a larger context of meaning and choice. This layer moves us from being passive recipients of life to active authors of it.

Tools for Reflection and Practice

1. **Meaning Map**: Write down the areas of life most important to you (relationships, work, creativity, service). Reflect on how each contributes to your sense of meaning.
2. **Values Compass**: Identify your top 5 core values. For each, write one action you can take this week to live more fully in alignment with it.
3. **Freedom and Responsibility Exercise**: Reflect on one area where you feel stuck. Ask yourself: 'What choices do I have here? What responsibility comes with those choices?'

4. **Legacy Letter**: Write a letter as if from your older self looking back. What do you hope to have stood for? What impact do you hope to leave?
5. **The Golden Rule Practice**: For one week, use the Golden Rule as a guiding principle in decisions, big or small. Notice how it shapes your relationships and sense of integrity.

Closing Reflection

The existential layer is where transformation becomes integration. At this depth, we are not simply managing habits, challenging beliefs, or uncovering repressed material; rather, we are choosing how to live. It is about meaning, purpose, freedom, and responsibility. Diego's moment on the beach illustrates this shift; he realized that beyond survival and self-improvement, life called him to define what truly matters.

Existential transformation is the invitation to become the author of your story, to align your life with values, and to live with the courage of authenticity. At this level, life is no longer about whether it is hard or easy. It becomes about whether it is lived meaningfully.

Belief-Feeling-Action Loop

References

- Deci, E. L., & Ryan, R. M. (2000). Self-determination theory and the facilitation of intrinsic motivation, social development, and well-being. American Psychologist, 55(1), 68–78.
- Frankl, V. E. (1959). Man's Search for Meaning. Beacon Press.
- Steger, M. F. (2009). Meaning in life. In S. J. Lopez (Ed.), Oxford Handbook of Positive Psychology (2nd ed., pp. 679–687). Oxford University Press.

Part III: From Effort to Integration

Chapter 8: The Spiral of Growth

For years, Aisha thought of growth as a straight line, as a path from struggle to success, from weakness to strength. But the more she reflected, the more she realized her journey was not linear at all. Each lesson seemed to circle back, presenting itself again in a new form, with new depth. When she changed her habits, old schemas resurfaced. When she worked through childhood wounds, new questions of meaning arose. It was as if she were moving in a spiral, revisiting familiar places, but never the same way twice. Each cycle took her deeper into awareness and higher into freedom. This is the spiral of growth.

A Conversation

Karen: *People often expect growth to be a straight line, but in reality, it's cyclical. We revisit the same themes — habits, schemas, wounds, meaning — but at new levels of awareness.*

Mardoche: *Exactly. It's like climbing a spiral staircase. From one angle, it looks like you're going in circles. But with each turn, you're actually ascending.*

Karen: *And this explains why people sometimes feel frustrated: 'Didn't I already deal with this?' The truth is, yes — but you're meeting it now with greater capacity.*

Mardoche: *Which is why integration is so important. Conscious, preconscious, unconscious, and existential layers aren't separate silos. They interconnect, reinforcing each other in a spiral of growth.*

The Science of Cyclical Growth

Developmental psychology recognizes growth as nonlinear. Erik Erikson's stages of psychosocial development, for example, recur in different forms throughout life. Challenges of trust, identity, and intimacy arise at multiple stages, each time offering a new layer of resolution (Erikson, 1950).

Neuroscience research shows that neural pathways strengthen through repeated activation. When individuals revisit similar challenges with new strategies, they reinforce healthy circuits and weaken unhealthy ones (Hebb, 1949; Doidge, 2007).

The spiral is also reflected in spiritual traditions. Many contemplative paths describe growth as a spiral of deepening awareness, where old lessons resurface until they are fully integrated. This reinforces the idea that growth is not about escaping cycles, but about embracing them at higher levels of consciousness.

Tools for Reflection and Practice

1. **Spiral Mapping**: Reflect on a recurring theme in your life (e.g., relationships, self-worth, career). Draw a spiral and mark the points where this theme reappeared. What new insights or capacities did you bring each time?
2. **Layered Challenge Exercise**: Take one current challenge and explore it across the four layers. Ask: How does this show up in my habits (conscious)? In my schemas (preconscious)? In my hidden wounds (unconscious)? In my search for meaning (existential)?
3. **Reframing Relapse**: Instead of viewing setbacks as failure, see them as part of the spiral. Ask: *'What am I learning this time that I couldn't before?'*
4. **Integration Journal**: At the end of each week, write one insight from each of the four layers. Notice how they interconnect and reinforce each other.

Closing Reflection

The spiral of growth teaches us patience and humility. We do not graduate from being human, nor do we ever finish learning. Instead, we revisit our struggles and joys with deeper awareness, greater compassion, and stronger integration. Aisha realized that every return to an old pattern was not regression but evolution, for the spiral pulling her higher. When we embrace the spiral, we see that growth is not about arriving, but about continuously deepening into the fullness of life.

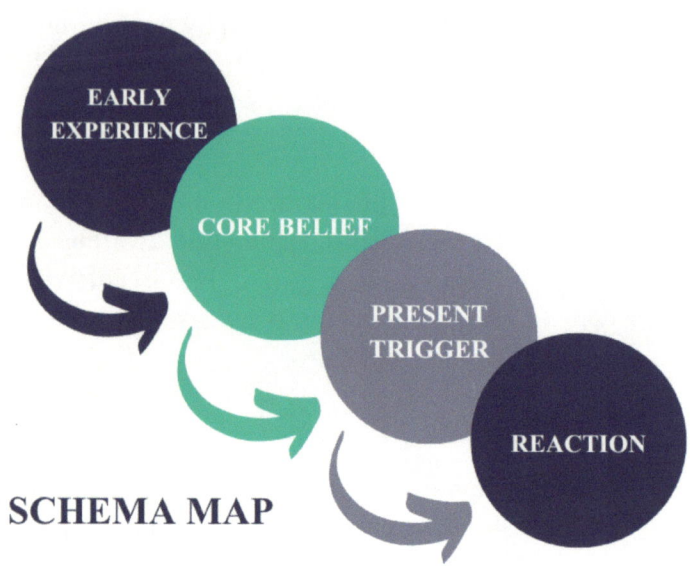

SCHEMA MAP

References

- Doidge, N. (2007). The Brain That Changes Itself: Stories of Personal Triumph from the Frontiers of Brain Science. Viking.
- Erikson, E. H. (1950). Childhood and Society. Norton.
- Hebb, D. O. (1949). The Organization of Behavior: A Neuropsychological Theory. Wiley.

Chapter 9: Life as Lightness

For most of his life, Rafael carried the belief that life was a burden. Work felt like obligation, relationships felt heavy with expectation, and even leisure carried guilt. However, one morning, while watching his daughter chase bubbles in the park, he noticed something striking: her laughter was effortless, her movement unforced, and her joy uncalculated. In that moment, Rafael realized that life did not have to feel so weighty; rather, it could be light, and not because responsibilities disappeared, but because the way he held them changed.

This chapter explores the shift from heaviness to lightness. Lightness is not about avoiding problems or pretending challenges don't exist. It is about living with a sense of presence, playfulness, and freedom, even in the midst of responsibility. It is about choosing how we carry life, rather than being crushed by it.

A Conversation

Karen: *When people think of lightness, they often confuse it with irresponsibility. However, that's not what we mean. Lightness is carrying responsibility without being consumed by it.*

Mardoche: *Exactly. It's like the difference between carrying a stone in your pocket and dragging a boulder on your back. The responsibilities may be the same, but your relationship to them is different.*

Karen: *And neuroscience shows us that states of flow, which is when people are deeply engaged in meaningful activity, are marked by effortlessness. Time feels different. The brain is both relaxed and focused (Csikszentmihalyi, 1990).*

Mardoche: *Which means lightness is not just an idea. It's a real psychological and physiological state. We can cultivate it by shifting attention, reframing struggle, and practicing presence.*

Karen: *And importantly, lightness is contagious. When leaders, parents, or clinicians embody it, they create environments where others can breathe easier too.*

The Science of Lightness

Flow research by Csikszentmihalyi (1990) demonstrates that people experience optimal states of engagement when challenges match skills. These moments are often described as light, timeless, and deeply fulfilling. Positive psychology further shows that cultivating joy, gratitude, and playfulness enhances resilience and well-being (Fredrickson, 2001).

Neuroscience reveals that stress and heaviness are linked to overactivation of the amygdala, while states of ease activate the parasympathetic nervous system, supporting relaxation and creativity (Sapolsky, 2004). Mindfulness practices, in particular, have been shown to reduce stress reactivity and increase feelings of spaciousness and lightness (Kabat-Zinn, 1990).

In sum, lightness is not about escaping reality. It is about rewiring our relationship to it, cultivating presence, flow, and perspective.

Tools for Reflection and Practice

1. **Lightness Lens**: At the start of each day, choose one responsibility and ask: *'How can I carry this with more ease today?'*
2. **Flow Activity**: Identify an activity where you lose track of time — playing music, gardening, writing, exercising. Schedule it at least once this week and notice the shift in your state of being.
3. **The Bubble Practice**: Spend five minutes watching something simple (like bubbles, trees swaying, or birds). Let yourself absorb its lightness. Carry that quality into the rest of your day.
4. **Reframe the Load**: Write down one task that feels heavy, and then reframe it: *'Instead of I have to, I get to…'* Notice how this subtle shift changes your experience.

5. **Shared Lightness**: Intentionally bring humor, play, or gentleness into one interaction each day. Observe how it impacts both you and the other person.

Closing Reflection

Life as lightness does not mean life without responsibility, pain, or complexity. It means carrying all of it differently, with more breath, perspective, and presence. Rafael realized that his daughter's laughter was not careless; rather, it was a reminder of a natural human state. We are not meant to live life under a constant weight; rather, we are meant to dance with it, flow with it, and carry it lightly.

When we embrace lightness, life becomes not only bearable, but beautiful; and it is no longer about whether life is hard or easy; rather, it is about whether we are willing to live with the grace of lightness.

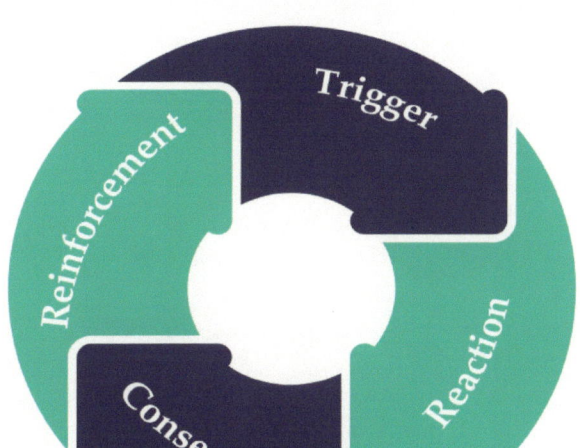

References

- Csikszentmihalyi, M. (1990). Flow: The Psychology of Optimal Experience. Harper & Row.
- Fredrickson, B. L. (2001). The role of positive emotions in positive psychology: The broaden-and-build theory of positive emotions. American Psychologist, 56(3), 218–226.
- Kabat-Zinn, J. (1990). Full Catastrophe Living: Using the Wisdom of Your Body and Mind to Face Stress, Pain, and Illness. Delacorte.
- Sapolsky, R. M. (2004). Why Zebras Don't Get Ulcers: The Acclaimed Guide to Stress, Stress-Related Diseases, and Coping. Holt Paperbacks.

Chapter 10: The Still Point

Elena often felt like her life was a pendulum, swinging between striving and exhaustion, between moments of joy and waves of despair. She longed for balance, but balance seemed like a distant ideal, forever just out of reach. One evening, while sitting quietly at her window, she noticed something remarkable. In the midst of the swinging, there was always a still point — the brief moment at the center of the pendulum's arc where movement paused before beginning again. In that instant, Elena realized that life's peace was not about stopping the swing, but about learning to rest in the still point within it.

This chapter is about discovering that still point — the place of presence and awareness that exists beneath the noise of life. It is not about erasing challenges or controlling every outcome, but about remembering that in every moment, there is a center we can return to.

A Conversation

Karen: *The still point is that moment of presence where we stop being pulled entirely by past regrets or future worries. It's where life is actually lived — here and now.*

Mardoche: *Yes, and many spiritual traditions describe this. T. S. Eliot wrote about 'the still point of the turning world,' where movement and stillness coexist. In psychology, mindfulness captures the same essence: the awareness of the present moment, without judgment.*

Karen: *And in neuroscience, when people practice mindfulness or breath awareness, the default mode network, the part of the brain that wanders into past and future, quiets down. This creates a sense of spaciousness and stillness (Brewer et al., 2011).*

Mardoche: *Which means the still point is not just a metaphor; rather, it's a real state we can access through attention and practice; and from that place, life feels less like a struggle and more like a flow.*

The Science of Presence and Stillness

Mindfulness research shows that present-moment awareness reduces anxiety, depression, and stress while increasing resilience and well-being (Kabat-Zinn, 1990; Davidson & Kaszniak, 2015). Practices like meditation and breath awareness activate the parasympathetic nervous system, slowing heart rate, lowering blood pressure, and calming the stress response.

Neuroimaging studies reveal that mindfulness decreases activity in the amygdala while enhancing connectivity in brain regions linked to emotional regulation (Hölzel et al., 2011). These physiological shifts explain why accessing a still point creates not only psychological calm but also physical healing.

Importantly, the still point is not about escaping reality. It is about grounding in reality more fully, experiencing life directly rather than through filters of worry, judgment, or distraction.

Tools for Reflection and Practice

1. **Breath Anchor**: Take three slow, deep breaths. With each inhale, notice the air entering. With each exhale, notice the release. Return to this whenever you feel pulled by stress or distraction.
2. **One-Minute Stillness**: Pause for one minute during your day. Simply notice your surroundings, your body, and your breath. Allow yourself to arrive fully in the present.
3. **Pendulum Reflection**: When life feels like it's swinging wildly, close your eyes and imagine the pendulum's still point. Ask yourself: *'Where is the calm center in this moment?'*
4. **Presence Journal**: Each evening, write down one moment when you felt present today. Reflect on how it changed your experience.
5. **The Golden Rule in Stillness**: Before responding to a conflict or challenge, pause at the still point. Ask: *'From this place of calm presence, how do I want to treat myself and others?'*

Closing Reflection

The still point is always available, though we often forget it in the rush of living. It is the space where movement meets stillness, where struggle dissolves into presence, and where meaning becomes clear. Elena discovered that she did not need to stop life's pendulum to find peace. She only needed to return, again and again, to the center within.

At the still point, life is no longer defined as hard or easy. It simply is, and in that simple being, we discover freedom, grace, and peace.

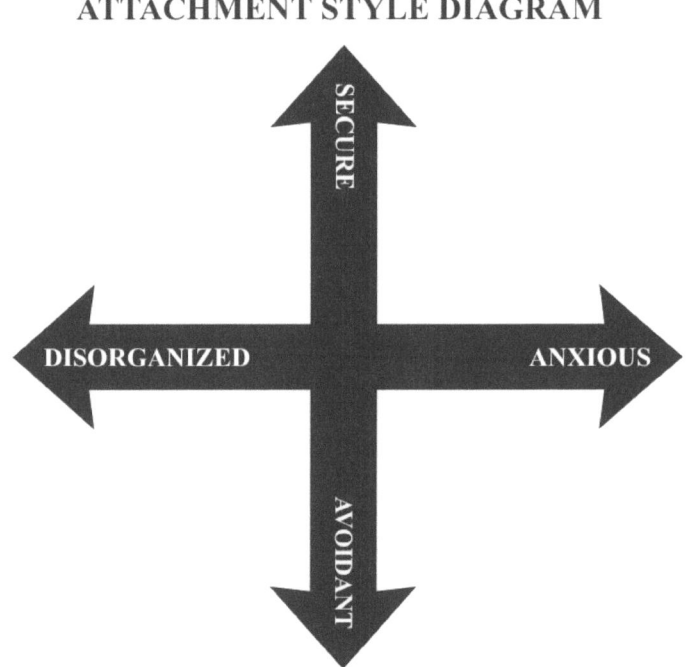

References

- Brewer, J. A., Worhunsky, P. D., Gray, J. R., Tang, Y. Y., Weber, J., & Kober, H. (2011). Meditation experience is associated with increased cortical thickness. NeuroReport, 22(17), 1–5.

- Davidson, R. J., & Kasczniak, A. W. (2015). Conceptual and methodological issues in research on mindfulness and meditation. American Psychologist, 70(7), 581–592.

- Hölzel, B. K., Lazar, S. W., Gard, T., Schuman-Olivier, Z., Vago, D. R., & Ott, U. (2011). How does mindfulness meditation work? Proposing mechanisms of action from a conceptual and neural perspective. Perspectives on Psychological Science, 6(6), 537–559.

- Kabat-Zinn, J. (1990). Full Catastrophe Living: Using the Wisdom of Your Body and Mind to Face Stress, Pain, and Illness. Delacorte.

Chapter 11: Everyday Integration – Living the Four Layers

When Malik first encountered the Four Layers of Transformation, it felt overwhelming. He wondered how anyone could possibly balance conscious habits, preconscious schemas, unconscious wounds, and existential choices all at once. However, as weeks passed, Malik realized something profound: integration didn't require perfection. It required practice — small, daily acts that wove the four layers together into the fabric of ordinary life.

This chapter is about bringing the layers down from theory into daily rhythm. It is about discovering how transformation becomes sustainable not in occasional breakthroughs, but in everyday living — in the way we wake up, relate, work, rest, and choose meaning.

A Conversation

Karen: *Integration sounds abstract until we make it practical. The question is: how do I live the Four Layers every day?*

Mardoche: *Yes. Let's break it down. At the conscious level, it's about habits — what time you wake, how you move your body, how you nourish yourself. These choices set the stage.*

Karen: *At the preconscious level, it's about noticing the patterns beneath those choices. If someone skips meals, is it just lack of time, a conscious decision to fast, or a schema of neglect resurfacing? Awareness of patterns deepens the work.*

Mardoche: *Then comes the unconscious. Dreams, slips of the tongue, and intense emotions reveal what still needs attention. By journaling, reflecting, or processing in therapy, we bring the hidden into the open.*

Karen: *And the existential layer asks: why does this matter? What am I choosing my life to stand for? When we align daily actions with meaning and values, everything integrates.*

Mardoche: *Exactly. Everyday integration is less about doing everything perfectly, and more about living with awareness across all four layers.*

The Science of Daily Integration

Behavioral science shows that habits shape identity over time. James Clear (2018) emphasizes that small, consistent actions compound, creating sustainable change. Neuroscience confirms this: repeated behaviors strengthen neural pathways (Hebb, 1949), turning conscious effort into automatic patterns.

Schema research (Young et al., 2003) demonstrates that awareness of recurring themes helps interrupt destructive cycles. Cognitive and acceptance-based therapies show that observing and labeling patterns reduces their control (Hayes et al., 1999).

Psychoanalytic and trauma research reveal that unconscious processes, including implicit memory, continue to influence behavior until brought into awareness (Schacter, 1996; van der Kolk, 2014). Finally, existential psychology emphasizes that a sense of meaning is essential for resilience and well-being (Frankl, 1959; Steger, 2009).

When woven together, these findings suggest that true integration happens when we live across all four layers, and not in isolation, but as a daily spiral of awareness and practice.

Tools for Reflection and Practice

1. **Four-Layer Check-In**: At the end of each day, reflect:
    a. Conscious – What habit supported me today?
    b. Preconscious – What pattern showed up?
    c. Unconscious – Did any dreams, slips, or strong emotions reveal something hidden?
    d. Existential – Did I act in alignment with my values?
2. **Integration Morning Ritual**: Begin the day with one small act for each layer — a stretch (conscious), an intention (preconscious), a journal note (unconscious), and a statement of purpose (existential).

3. **Weekly Spiral Map**: Choose one theme (e.g., self-worth, relationships, work stress). Map how it appears at each layer. This helps you see the interconnectedness of growth.

4. **Embodied Reminder**: Wear a bracelet, ring, or keep a small object with you. Each time you see it, pause to ask: *'Am I living across all four layers right now?'*

5. **Integration Partner**: Share your reflections with a trusted friend or mentor once a week. Discuss how each of you is practicing daily integration.

Closing Reflection

Everyday integration is not about adding more tasks to an already full life. It is about shifting how we live the life we already have. Malik discovered that by weaving small practices into his day, aligning habits, noticing patterns, exploring hidden material, and choosing meaning, life began to feel less fragmented. It felt whole.

The Four Layers of Transformation are not abstract theories. They are living practices, available in every breath and every choice. When we practice them daily, life stops being divided into 'hard' and 'easy.' It becomes integrated, meaningful, and alive.

References

- Clear, J. (2018). Atomic Habits: An Easy & Proven Way to Build Good Habits & Break Bad Ones. Avery.
- Frankl, V. E. (1959). Man's Search for Meaning. Beacon Press.
- Hayes, S. C., Strosahl, K., & Wilson, K. G. (1999). Acceptance and Commitment Therapy: An Experiential Approach to Behavior Change. Guilford Press.
- Hebb, D. O. (1949). The Organization of Behavior: A Neuropsychological Theory. Wiley.
- Schacter, D. L. (1996). Searching for Memory: The Brain, the Mind, and the Past. Basic Books.
- Steger, M. F. (2009). Meaning in life. In S. J. Lopez (Ed.), Oxford Handbook of Positive Psychology (2nd ed., pp. 679–687). Oxford University Press.
- van der Kolk, B. A. (2014). The Body Keeps the Score: Brain, Mind, and Body in the Healing of Trauma. Viking.
- Young, J. E., Klosko, J. S., & Weishaar, M. E. (2003). Schema Therapy: A Practitioner's Guide. Guilford Press.

Chapter 12: From Effort to Embodiment

At first, transformation feels like effort. Leila set reminders on her phone to meditate, forced herself to track her habits, and wrote self-affirming statements on sticky notes all over her apartment. Change required constant willpower, and at times she wondered if it would always feel like pushing a boulder uphill. However, months later, something shifted. She no longer had to remind herself to breathe deeply when stressed, for her body did it automatically. Her evenings of journaling no longer felt like discipline; rather, they became something she looked forward to. What began as effort had turned into embodiment.

This chapter explores the movement from external effort to internal embodiment — when practices stop being things we do and become part of who we are. It is the difference between performing change and living it, between discipline imposed from outside and transformation arising from within.

A Conversation

Karen: *In the beginning, effort is necessary. You have to consciously disrupt old habits and build new ones. However, if change stays only at the level of effort, it eventually exhausts people.*

Mardoche: *Exactly. That's why embodiment matters. Neuroscience shows that repeated actions become automatic as neural pathways strengthen. It's what Hebb called, 'neurons that fire together, wire together' (Hebb, 1949).*

Karen: *And it's not just about habits. At the existential layer, embodiment means living from values so consistently that they become your natural compass. You don't ask, 'What should I do?' You act from who you are.*

Mardoche: *Which means real transformation feels lighter over time. The boulder doesn't disappear, but you discover it has wheels, and eventually, you realize you've become strong enough to carry it with ease.*

The Science of Embodiment

Research on habit formation suggests that consistent repetition over time shifts behaviors from effortful control to automaticity (Lally et al., 2010). This process reflects neuroplasticity: the brain's ability to rewire itself in response to repeated experience (Doidge, 2007).

Mind-body practices highlight embodiment as well. Studies of mindfulness, yoga, and breath awareness show that these practices become more effective the longer they are sustained, with physiological changes including reduced stress reactivity, improved heart-rate variability, and greater emotional regulation (Kabat-Zinn, 1990; Streeter et al., 2012).

At the existential level, self-determination theory (Deci & Ryan, 2000) demonstrates that when behaviors align with intrinsic motivation and values, they are more likely to become embodied and sustainable. In short: effort begins the process, but embodiment secures it.

Tools for Reflection and Practice

1. **Effort vs. Embodiment Journal**: Reflect on one change you are working on. Which parts still require effort? Which parts feel natural now?
2. **Embodiment Visualization**: Imagine yourself five years from now, living your values fully. What does your day look like? What feels natural? What feels light?
3. **Body Awareness Practice**: Spend five minutes noticing how your body responds to a chosen practice (breath awareness, journaling, exercise). Ask: *'Is this becoming part of me?'*

4. **Automaticity Tracker**: Notice which habits you no longer think about — the ones that happen naturally. Celebrate these as signs of embodiment.
5. **Value Alignment Audit**: Choose one decision today and ask: 'Am I choosing this from effort, or from embodiment of my values?'

Closing Reflection

Transformation begins with effort, but its true power unfolds in embodiment. Leila's journey illustrates that the practices we once strain to maintain can become the very rhythms that carry us. Effort builds the bridge, but embodiment allows us to live on the other side. When transformation becomes embodied, life stops feeling like a project to manage and begins to feel like a life to live. This is the shift from 'trying' to 'being,' and it is where lightness, integration, and freedom truly begin.

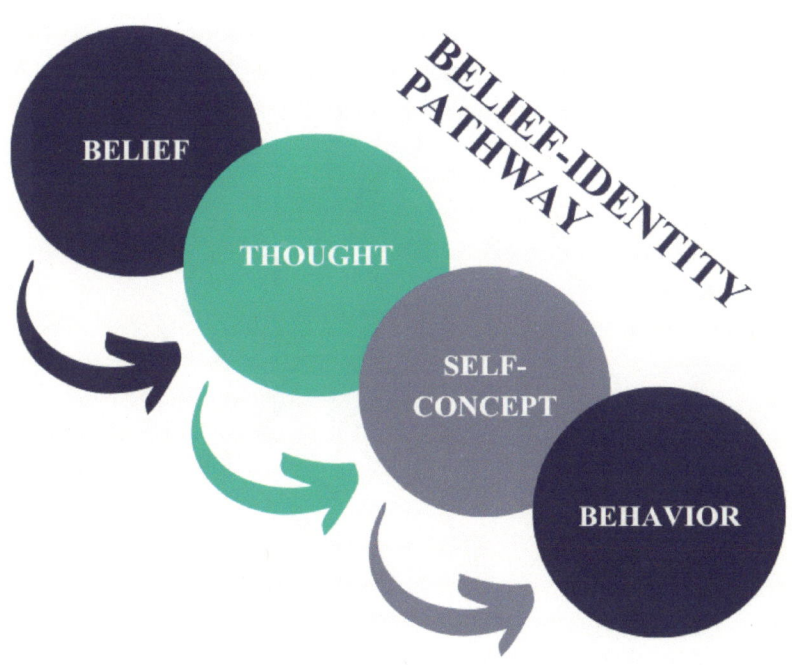

References

- Deci, E. L., & Ryan, R. M. (2000). Self-determination theory and the facilitation of intrinsic motivation, social development, and well-being. American Psychologist, 55(1), 68–78.
- Doidge, N. (2007). The Brain That Changes Itself: Stories of Personal Triumph from the Frontiers of Brain Science. Viking.
- Hebb, D. O. (1949). The Organization of Behavior: A Neuropsychological Theory. Wiley.
- Kabat-Zinn, J. (1990). Full Catastrophe Living: Using the Wisdom of Your Body and Mind to Face Stress, Pain, and Illness. Delacorte.
- Lally, P., van Jaarsveld, C. H., Potts, H. W., & Wardle, J. (2010). How are habits formed: Modelling habit formation in the real world. European Journal of Social Psychology, 40(6), 998–1009.
- Streeter, C. C., et al. (2012). Effects of yoga on the autonomic nervous system, gamma-aminobutyric-acid, and allostasis in epilepsy, depression, and post-traumatic stress disorder. Medical Hypotheses, 78(5), 571–579.

Chapter 13: The Dance of Wholeness

For Sofia, transformation once felt like a checklist: meditate daily, journal, practice gratitude, attend therapy, eat healthier, sleep more. Each practice helped, but she still felt fragmented, as if her life were divided into compartments, each managed separately. Then, during a weekend retreat, she joined a movement meditation. As she swayed to the music, eyes closed, she felt her breath, her emotions, her memories, and her sense of purpose converge into a single flow. For the first time, she felt whole. This was not about balance as a static state; rather, it was a dance, a living and moving wholeness that embraced all parts of her.

A Conversation

Karen: *Wholeness is not about perfection; rather, it's about integration, honoring every part of ourselves, even the messy ones.*

Mardoche: *Exactly. Too often, people think wholeness means eliminating flaws or contradictions. Real wholeness is like a dance, and it's fluid, dynamic, always shifting, yet grounded in harmony.*

Karen: *And the dance metaphor is important because it highlights movement. Wholeness isn't static; rather, we're constantly adjusting, listening, and responding to the rhythm of life.*

Mardoche: *Research on complexity and resilience shows that systems thrive not through rigidity, but through flexibility and adaptation (Holling, 2001). The same is true for us.*

The Science of Wholeness and Integration

Systems theory and complexity science reveal that resilience emerges from integration. Rigid systems break under pressure, while flexible systems adapt and evolve (Holling, 2001). Self-determination theory also shows that well-being arises when autonomy, competence, and relatedness are integrated into daily life (Deci & Ryan, 2000).

Mind-body research highlights that practices which unify breath, movement, and awareness, such as yoga and tai chi, foster psychological and physiological coherence (Streeter et al., 2012). Neuroscience further demonstrates that integration across brain networks is associated with greater well-being and adaptability (Siegel, 2012).

In short, wholeness is less about eliminating contradictions and more about dancing with them, aligning body, mind, emotions, and values into a living flow.

Tools for Reflection and Practice

1. **Wholeness Inventory**: List the parts of yourself you celebrate and the parts you resist. Ask: *'How might all of these belong in my dance of wholeness?'*

2. **Movement Practice**: Put on music and let your body move without choreography. Notice how emotions and thoughts arise and integrate through movement.

3. **Daily Integration Pause**: Three times a day, stop and ask: 'Am I fragmented or integrated right now? What would bring me into wholeness?'

4. **Harmony Journal**: At the end of each day, write one moment when you felt whole — even if just for a second. Reflect on what made it possible.

5. **Embracing Contradictions**: Choose one area where you feel divided (e.g., wanting independence and closeness). Explore how both can coexist in your dance of wholeness.

Closing Reflection

The dance of wholeness is not about arriving at a perfect state. It is about learning to move with all of life's rhythms — joy and sorrow, effort and ease, fear and courage. Sofia's experience showed her that wholeness was not something to achieve, but something to embody. In the dance, she discovered a harmony that could not be forced, only felt.

When we stop trying to control every step and instead listen to the rhythm of life, we realize that we are already whole. Wholeness is not a goal; rather, it is the dance itself.

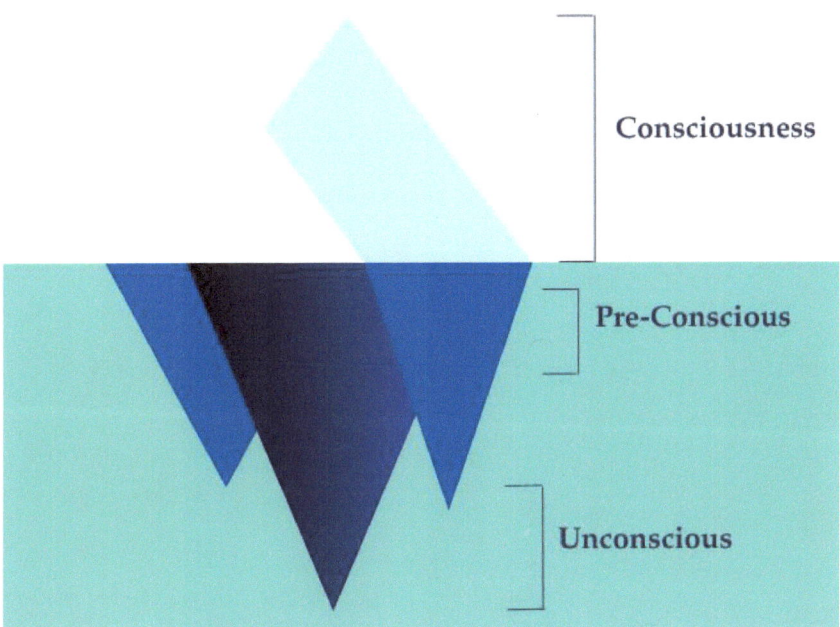

References

- Deci, E. L., & Ryan, R. M. (2000). Self-determination theory and the facilitation of intrinsic motivation, social development, and well-being. American Psychologist, 55(1), 68–78.

- Holling, C. S. (2001). Understanding the complexity of economic, ecological, and social systems. Ecosystems, 4(5), 390–405.

- Siegel, D. J. (2012). The Developing Mind: How Relationships and the Brain Interact to Shape Who We Are (2nd ed.). Guilford Press.

- Streeter, C. C., et al. (2012). Effects of yoga on the autonomic nervous system, gamma-aminobutyric-acid, and allostasis in epilepsy, depression, and post-traumatic stress disorder. Medical Hypotheses, 78(5), 571–579.

Chapter 14: Habits of Ease – Structuring a Life That Flows

When Daniel looked at his calendar, he often felt suffocated. Every hour was filled with tasks, meetings, and deadlines. His life was structured, but the structure felt like a cage. Then, after a period of burnout, he decided to redesign his days with a new intention: ease. He began waking up earlier, not to get more done, but to sit quietly with his coffee. He scheduled short breaks for stretching, breathing, and simply looking out the window. To his surprise, his productivity increased, his stress decreased, and his sense of life shifted. Daniel had discovered that the right habits, intentionally structured, could create a life that flowed instead of one that drained.

A Conversation

Karen: *People often resist structure because they associate it with rigidity. However, structure, when built with awareness, can create freedom.*

Mardoche: *Yes, think of a river. Without banks, water spreads chaotically. However, with banks, it flows powerfully in a direction. Structure is the container that allows life to flow with ease.*

Karen: *The key is designing habits that support, not suffocate. Research shows that even small rituals can create a sense of rhythm that reduces stress.*

Mardoche: *And these habits don't have to be grand. Micro-habits, like a two-minute pause for breath awareness, shift physiology and psychology profoundly when practiced consistently.*

The Science of Habits and Flow

Habits free up cognitive energy by automating behavior, allowing the brain to focus on higher-order tasks (Duhigg, 2012; Clear, 2018). Neuroscience shows that habits are encoded in the basal ganglia, making repeated behaviors more efficient over time (Graybiel, 2008).

Research on flow (Csikszentmihalyi, 1990) highlights the importance of balancing challenge and skill. When daily structures reduce overwhelm and provide rhythm, individuals are more likely to enter flow states, where effort feels effortless and productivity is maximized.

Physiological studies demonstrate that micro-practices like mindful breathing and short breaks regulate the autonomic nervous system, reducing cortisol and increasing resilience (Kabat-Zinn, 1990; Davidson & Kaszniak, 2015).

In essence, structuring life with habits of ease creates conditions where flow becomes natural rather than forced.

Tools for Reflection and Practice

1. **Morning Anchor**: Begin your day with one habit that grounds you (stretching, journaling, quiet reflection). This sets the tone for flow.

2. **Micro-Break Ritual**: Every two hours, pause for 2–3 minutes. Breathe deeply, stretch, or notice your surroundings. These pauses reset your nervous system.

3. **Ease Audit**: Review your daily schedule. Highlight tasks that feel draining. Ask: *'Can I approach this with more lightness or restructure it for ease?'*

4. **Flow Hour**: Block one hour each day for deep, uninterrupted work on something meaningful. Notice how creating structure supports creativity.

5. **Evening Closure**: End your day with a reflection practice — write down three things you are grateful for, and one way you lived with ease.

Closing Reflection

Habits of ease are not about avoiding responsibility, but about carrying it with lightness. Daniel discovered that structure, when consciously designed, did not confine him; rather, it liberated him. The paradox is that freedom is not found in chaos but in flow, and flow is created by supportive rhythms. When we build habits of ease, life stops feeling like an endless climb and begins to feel like a river — steady, alive, and moving forward.

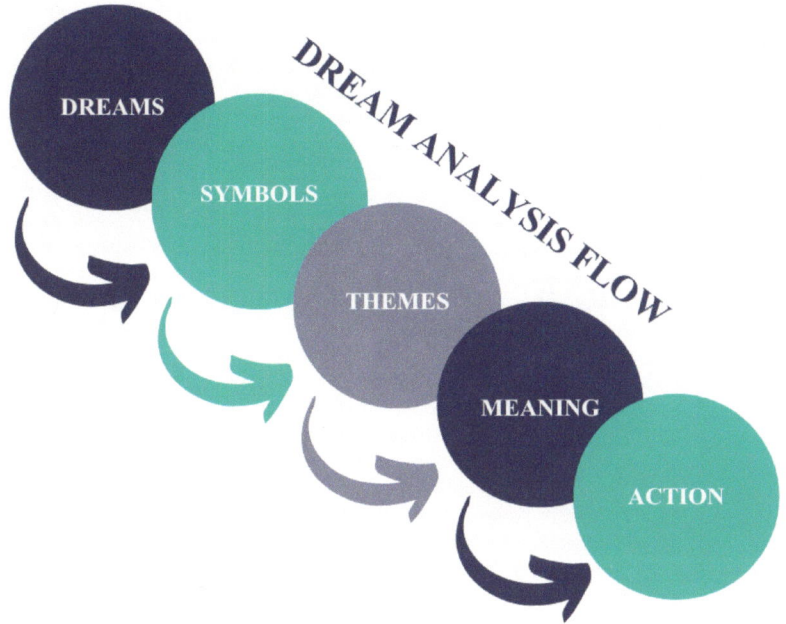

References

- Clear, J. (2018). Atomic Habits: An Easy & Proven Way to Build Good Habits & Break Bad Ones. Avery.
- Csikszentmihalyi, M. (1990). Flow: The Psychology of Optimal Experience. Harper & Row.
- Davidson, R. J., & KasFzniak, A. W. (2015). Conceptual and methodological issues in research on mindfulness and meditation. American Psychologist, 70(7), 581–592.
- Duhigg, C. (2012). The Power of Habit: Why We Do What We Do in Life and Business. Random House.
- Graybiel, A. M. (2008). Habits, rituals, and the evaluative brain. Annual Review of Neuroscience, 31, 359–387.
- Kabat-Zinn, J. (1990). Full Catastrophe Living: Using the Wisdom of Your Body and Mind to Face Stress, Pain, and Illness. Delacorte.

Chapter 15: Resilience Without Struggle

When Jonah thought of resilience, he imagined soldiers enduring battle, athletes training through pain, and survivors overcoming unimaginable hardships. Resilience, to him, was forged in fire. But his perspective shifted when he met Rosa, a 78-year-old gardener in his neighborhood. Rosa radiated calm strength, not because she had fought endless battles, but because she lived with joy, curiosity, and deep connection. She reminded Jonah that resilience was not always about surviving storms, and that sometimes it was about cultivating roots in rich soil. Resilience, he realized, did not have to be born from struggle; rather, it could also grow from love, presence, and daily practices that nurtured well-being.

A Conversation

Karen: *People often equate resilience with hardship, as though we must suffer to be strong. But that's not the whole story.*

Mardoche: *Exactly. Research on protective factors shows that resilience is just as much about what supports us as what challenges us. A strong social network, mindfulness, and meaning-making are resilience builders that don't require trauma.*

Karen: *That reframes resilience beautifully. It's not just bouncing back from adversity; rather, it's also about bouncing forward through joy, love, and purpose.*

Mardoche: *And this matters because if we teach people resilience only through the lens of struggle, we unintentionally reinforce the myth that life has to be hard in order to have value, for resilience can also be gentle, cultivated, and life-affirming.*

The Science of Resilience Beyond Struggle

Resilience has traditionally been studied in the context of adversity, but research now highlights the role of positive experiences in building strength. Ann Masten (2001) coined the term 'ordinary magic' to describe the everyday factors, such as secure relationships, routines, supportive communities, that create resilience.

Fredrickson's broaden-and-build theory (2001) demonstrates that positive emotions such as joy, gratitude, and love expand awareness, build resources, and enhance coping capacity. These experiences prepare individuals to face challenges with greater flexibility and creativity.

Neuroscience research also shows that resilience is linked to neuroplasticity. Practices such as mindfulness meditation strengthen brain networks involved in emotional regulation, stress recovery, and perspective-taking (Davidson & McEwen, 2012).

Together, this evidence suggests that resilience does not need to be forged solely through suffering. It can be cultivated through intentional practices, nurturing environments, and life-affirming choices.

Tools for Reflection and Practice

1. **Joy Journal**: Record one joyful moment each day. Over time, you will see how joy itself builds resilience.

2. **Connection Map**: Write down your circle of support — friends, mentors, community members. Notice how these connections provide strength even outside of struggle.

3. **Resilience Ritual**: Choose one daily practice (mindfulness, breath awareness, gratitude, or movement) to anchor your nervous system and build resilience over time.

4. **Bounce-Forward Reflection**: Think of a recent challenge. Ask: 'What strength or resource helped me not just survive, but grow?' Identify how this resource can be nurtured without waiting for hardship.

5. **Gentle Exposure**: Instead of waiting for crises, create small, manageable challenges that stretch you, such as learning a new skill, traveling, or speaking up in a meeting, to build resilience through growth, not trauma.

Closing Reflection

Resilience is not only the capacity to endure storms; rather, it is also the ability to dance in the sunlight, to grow roots in fertile ground, and to expand through joy. Rosa embodied resilience not because she survived endless suffering, but because she cultivated habits of presence, connection, and gratitude that sustained her. Jonah realized that resilience without struggle was not only possible; rather, it was profoundly powerful, and when we redefine resilience as something that can be grown gently and joyfully, we free ourselves from the myth that life must be hard. Resilience, then, becomes not a badge of survival, but a way of living with strength, ease, and grace.

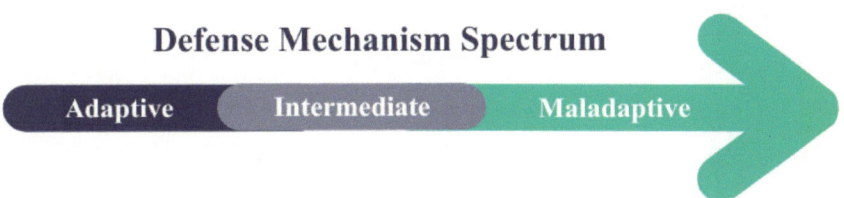

References

- Davidson, R. J., & McEwen, B. S. (2012). Social influences on neuroplasticity: Stress and interventions to promote well-being. Nature Neuroscience, 15(5), 689–695.
- Fredrickson, B. L. (2001). The role of positive emotions in positive psychology: The broaden-and-build theory of positive emotions. American Psychologist, 56(3), 218–226.
- Masten, A. S. (2001). Ordinary magic: Resilience processes in development. American Psychologist, 56(3), 227–238.

Chapter 16: Love Without Hardness

When Maya thought of love, she thought of sacrifice, compromise, and pain. Her parents had modeled love as endurance, which meant staying together despite constant conflict. Her friends often described love as 'hard work.' And in her own relationships, Maya found herself bracing for struggle, as if love without hardship wasn't real. However, one evening, sitting quietly with her partner, sipping tea in companionable silence, she realized something new: love could be gentle, nourishing, and even effortless. It did not have to be hard to be true. This was a revelation, that love, at its essence, is not meant to weigh us down but to lift us up.

A Conversation

Karen: *We've been taught that love has to be hard and full of sacrifice, compromise, and endless effort. But what if that's not true?*

Mardoche: *Yes, love does require attention and presence, and when it's aligned with values and mutual care, it doesn't feel like a battle; rather, it feels like flow.*

Karen: *And attachment science is helpful here. Secure love isn't marked by constant conflict; rather, it's marked by safety, playfulness, and trust; and hardness often comes from old schemas and wounds, and not from love itself.*

Mardoche: *Exactly. If someone carries a schema of abandonment or mistrust, relationships will feel harder than they need to. Healing those patterns opens the possibility for love to feel lighter and freer.*

Karen: *Which is why part of the work of love is self-work. When we shift at the conscious, preconscious, and unconscious layers, we make room for existential love, the kind that is rooted in meaning and freedom, not fear and struggle.*

The Science of Love Without Hardness

Attachment research demonstrates that secure relationships are characterized by safety, responsiveness, and mutual support (Bowlby, 1969; Ainsworth, 1978). These bonds allow individuals to explore and grow, knowing they can return to a safe base.

Psychological studies reveal that love grounded in positive emotions broadens awareness and builds enduring resources (Fredrickson, 2001). Couples who cultivate shared joy, gratitude, and humor show higher resilience and satisfaction (Gottman & Silver, 1999).

Neuroscience research shows that oxytocin, sometimes called the 'bonding hormone,' is released through touch, trust, and connection, creating feelings of warmth and safety (Carter, 1998). This biological foundation suggests that love, at its core, is designed to soothe, and not to strain.

While conflict and effort are sometimes part of relationships, they do not define love. Love can be, and is meant to be a source of lightness, nourishment, and growth.

Tools for Reflection and Practice

1. **Love Audit**: Reflect on your beliefs about love. Do you see it as 'hard work'? Where did that belief come from?

2. **Secure Base Practice**: With your partner, create rituals of safety — daily check-ins, shared gratitude, or simple moments of affection.

3. **Schema Awareness**: Notice when old fears (abandonment, mistrust, unworthiness) show up in your relationships. Label them as patterns, and not truth.

4. **Joyful Connection**: Intentionally add play and humor into your relationships. Laughter builds bonds and reduces stress.

5. **Existential Love Reflection**: Ask yourself, 'How does my love reflect my deepest values? How do I want my love to shape the world around me?'

Closing Reflection

Love without hardness is not love without depth; rather, it is love that flows from safety, trust, and alignment. Maya discovered that love didn't have to feel like endurance; rather, it could feel like breathing, like resting, and like coming home. True love does not demand that we suffer to prove it is real. It invites us to grow, to play, and to share life with lightness. When we free love from the myth of hardness, we discover its essence: a force that nourishes, uplifts, and expands both self and other.

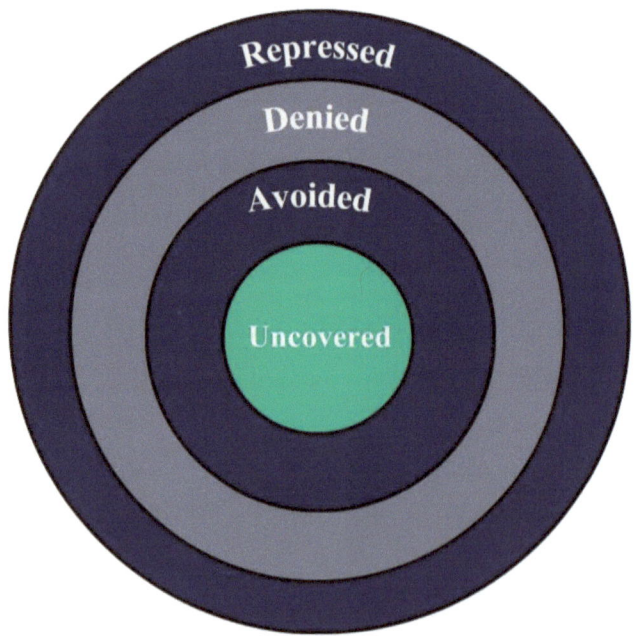

Unconscious Vault Diagram

References

- Ainsworth, M. D. S. (1978). Patterns of Attachment: A Psychological Study of the Strange Situation. Lawrence Erlbaum Associates.

- Bowlby, J. (1969). Attachment and Loss: Vol. 1. Attachment. Basic Books.

- Carter, C. S. (1998). Neuroendocrine perspectives on social attachment and love. Psychoneuroendocrinology, 23(8), 779–818.

- Fredrickson, B. L. (2001). The role of positive emotions in positive psychology: The broaden-and-build theory of positive emotions. American Psychologist, 56(3), 218–226.

- Gottman, J., & Silver, N. (1999). The Seven Principles for Making Marriage Work. Crown.

Chapter 17: Parenting with Lightness

For years, Thomas believed that being a good parent meant constant worry. He thought love was measured by sleepless nights, strict discipline, and endless sacrifice. Parenting, in his mind, was supposed to be hard. However, one afternoon, while watching his daughter build a tower of blocks, he noticed something: she was learning not through lectures or punishments, but through play. Her joy was her teacher, and in that moment, Thomas realized that parenting did not need to be defined by strain and anxiety; rather, it could be guided by lightness, and a way of holding responsibility with love, curiosity, and presence.

A Conversation

Karen: *Many parents believe they must carry the weight of the world on their shoulders. But children often learn best when parenting is infused with lightness.*

Mardoche: *Exactly. Research on attachment shows that children thrive when caregivers are consistent and responsive, not when they're anxious or overly controlling.*

Karen: *And lightness doesn't mean neglect; rather, it means modeling resilience, joy, and presence; and when parents embody those qualities, children absorb them naturally.*

Mardoche: *Yes, and play is central here. Neuroscience shows that play activates learning pathways in the brain, strengthening problem-solving, creativity, and emotional regulation. Parenting with lightness means making room for play, both for the child and the parent.*

The Science of Parenting with Lightness

Attachment theory demonstrates that children need a secure base, and that is, caregivers who provide safety, comfort, and encouragement (Bowlby, 1969; Ainsworth, 1978). This foundation allows children to explore the world with confidence.

Developmental psychology emphasizes the role of play in growth. Play fosters creativity, problem-solving, and social-emotional development (Brown & Vaughan, 2009). Far from being frivolous, play is one of the most powerful forms of learning.

Parental stress, however, can disrupt this process. Studies show that high parental anxiety can transmit stress to children, undermining their emotional well-being (Waters et al., 2017). Conversely, mindfulness-based parenting reduces stress, increases patience, and enhances parent-child connection (Bögels et al., 2010).

Together, this evidence suggests that lightness in parenting is not only beneficial but essential. It creates a home where children and parents alike can thrive.

Tools for Reflection and Practice

1. **Play Prescription**: Dedicate 15 minutes daily to unstructured play with your child. Follow their lead without agenda.

2. **Parenting Pause**: When stress arises, take three breaths before responding. This models emotional regulation and creates space for more thoughtful reactions.

3. **Joy Journal with Children**: Each night, share with your child one joyful moment from the day. Invite them to do the same.

4. **Secure Base Rituals**: Create consistent practices that signal safety — morning hugs, bedtime stories, or family meals.

5. **Self-Compassion Practice**: Remember that lightness starts with the parent. Treat yourself with the same gentleness you offer your child.

Closing Reflection

Parenting with lightness is not about avoiding responsibility; rather, it is about carrying it differently, with presence, joy, and trust. Thomas discovered that his daughter didn't need him to be perfect or perpetually worried. She needed him to be present, responsive, and playful. When we release the myth that parenting must always be hard, we make room for connection, growth, and joy. Parenting becomes not only a responsibility but also a gift, and a chance to rediscover lightness through the eyes of a child.

References

- Ainsworth, M. D. S. (1978). Patterns of Attachment: A Psychological Study of the Strange Situation. Lawrence Erlbaum Associates.

- Bögels, S. M., et al. (2010). Mindfulness in the parenting context. In F. Didonna (Ed.), Clinical Handbook of Mindfulness (pp. 439–455). Springer.

- Bowlby, J. (1969). Attachment and Loss: Vol. 1. Attachment. Basic Books.

- Brown, S., & Vaughan, C. (2009). Play: How It Shapes the Brain, Opens the Imagination, and Invigorates the Soul. Avery.

- Waters, S. F., West, T. V., & Mendes, W. B. (2017). Stress contagion: Physiological covariation between mothers and infants. Psychological Science, 25(4), 934–942.

Chapter 18: Friendship, Belonging, and Joy

Elena had always considered herself independent. She prided herself on handling challenges alone, believing that resilience meant self-sufficiency. However, after moving to a new city, she began to feel the ache of loneliness. Her evenings stretched long and empty, and her successes felt hollow without someone to share them with. She, then, slowly, began forming new friendships with, neighbors who invited her for tea, colleagues who checked in on her, and a community group where she found laughter and connection. Elena realized something essential: resilience and joy were not built alone; rather, they were nurtured in belonging, in shared laughter, and in the lightness of friendship.

A Conversation

Karen: *Friendship and belonging are often underestimated in discussions of well-being. Yet, research shows that they are among the strongest predictors of happiness and health.*

Mardoche: *Yes, the Harvard Study of Adult Development found that the quality of relationships is more important for longevity and well-being than wealth, fame, or even genetics.*

Karen: *And friendship doesn't have to be complicated. Shared laughter, simple rituals, and genuine presence create bonds that sustain us.*

Mardoche: *Exactly. Belonging is a basic human need. When people feel connected, their stress decreases, their health improves, and their resilience grows. Belonging itself is medicine.*

The Science of Friendship and Belonging

Decades of research reveal that social connection is a critical determinant of health. The Harvard Study of Adult Development, one of the longest-running studies on human well-being, found that close relationships predict happiness and longevity more than income, IQ, or social class (Waldinger & Schulz, 2010).

Social neuroscience reveals that human brains are wired for connection. Positive interactions release oxytocin, reduce cortisol, and strengthen immune function (Carter, 1998). Conversely, chronic loneliness is linked to increased risk of depression, cardiovascular disease, and mortality (Holt-Lunstad et al., 2010).

Belonging also fosters joy. Fredrickson's broaden-and-build theory (2001) highlights that shared positive emotions expand awareness, enhance creativity, and build enduring resources. Simply put, friendship and belonging are not luxuries, they are essential to human flourishing.

Tools for Reflection and Practice

1. **Friendship Audit**: List the people in your life who bring you joy and those who drain your energy. Commit to nurturing the former.

2. **Ritual of Connection**: Establish small, regular rituals with friends — weekly calls, monthly dinners, or daily check-ins.

3. **Belonging Map**: Reflect on where you feel a sense of belonging (family, community, groups). Notice where this is missing and consider how you might create it.

4. **Acts of Friendship**: Each week, reach out to one person with a small act of kindness — a text, a note, or a gesture of support.

5. **Joyful Gatherings**: Plan or join activities centered around shared joy — games, meals, walks, or creative projects. Notice how joy multiplies when shared.

Closing Reflection

Friendship, belonging, and joy are not side notes to life. They are central to well-being and resilience. Elena discovered that independence may be admirable, but it is interdependence that sustains us. Through belonging, we find strength; through friendship, we find laughter; and through joy, we find meaning. Life does not have to be carried alone; rather, it is meant to be shared, and in that sharing, hardship softens, and joy expands.

References

- Carter, C. S. (1998). Neuroendocrine perspectives on social attachment and love. Psychoneuroendocrinology, 23(8), 779–818.
- Fredrickson, B. L. (2001). The role of positive emotions in positive psychology: The broaden-and-build theory of positive emotions. American Psychologist, 56(3), 218–226.
- Holt-Lunstad, J., Smith, T. B., & Layton, J. B. (2010). Social relationships and mortality risk: A meta-analytic review. PLoS Medicine, 7(7), e1000316.
- Waldinger, R. J., & Schulz, M. S. (2010). The Harvard Study of Adult Development: Lessons from a 75-year study of happiness. Harvard Medical School.

Chapter 19: Work and Service as Play

For many years, Jordan approached work as duty. He measured success in long hours, missed vacations, and the exhaustion he carried home each evening. Service, too, felt heavy, as something he gave to others only by draining himself. However, his perspective shifted when he joined a community project to build a neighborhood garden. There, he noticed something surprising: he wasn't exhausted; rather, he was energized, working alongside neighbors, laughing, planting, and creating together. He felt a sense of flow, and for the first time, he realized that work and service did not have to feel like burdens; rather, they could feel like play and expressions of creativity, connection, and joy.

A Conversation

Karen: *Many people equate work with struggle, as if effort and exhaustion prove its value; but that mindset robs us of the joy that work and service can bring.*

Mardoche: *Exactly. When work is aligned with strengths and values, it feels more like play than punishment. Mihaly Csikszentmihalyi's research on flow shows that people are most fulfilled when they're deeply engaged in meaningful activity.*

Karen: *And service, too, can be playful. True service isn't about depletion; rather, it's about giving in ways that also nourish us.*

Mardoche: *Which means reframing both work and service. Instead of asking, 'How much did I sacrifice?' we can ask, 'How much did I create, connect, and play?'*

Karen: *That shift allows us to see work and service not as hard obligations but as opportunities for joy and transformation.*

The Science of Work, Service, and Play

Research on flow (Csikszentmihalyi, 1990) shows that people experience deep satisfaction when challenges match skills, creating states where work feels effortless and fulfilling. These experiences are often described as playful, even in serious contexts.

Positive psychology highlights that aligning work with strengths increases engagement, productivity, and well-being (Seligman, 2011). When individuals use their natural talents, work becomes less about effort and more about expression.

Studies on service demonstrate that giving to others enhances happiness, health, and even longevity (Post, 2005); and the benefits are greatest when service is voluntary, meaningful, and connected to joy rather than obligation.

Together, this research suggests that reframing work and service as play not only reduces stress but also maximizes creativity, connection, and resilience.

Tools for Reflection and Practice

1. **Flow Journal**: At the end of each week, record one moment when work felt like play. Notice the conditions that made this possible.

2. **Strength Alignment**: Identify your top strengths (creativity, empathy, leadership, problem-solving). Find one way to use them more fully in your work or service.

3. **Service Reframe**: Reflect on one act of service. Instead of asking, 'What did it cost me?' ask, 'How did it nourish me and others?'

4. **Play Infusion**: Bring elements of play into your workday — humor, curiosity, experimentation. Notice how this shifts your energy.

5. **Meaning Map**: Write down how your work and service connect to your larger values and purpose. Let this meaning reframe effort into joy.

Closing Reflection

Work and service are not meant to drain us; rather, they are meant to engage, energize, and connect us. Jordan discovered that when he approached his garden project not as obligation but as play, everything shifted, including, his energy, his joy, and his sense of purpose. When we reframe work and service as opportunities for creativity and connection, life becomes less about endurance and more about play; and in that play, we discover the lightness of living with meaning.

References

- Csikszentmihalyi, M. (1990). Flow: The Psychology of Optimal Experience. Harper & Row.

- Post, S. G. (2005). Altruism, happiness, and health: It's good to be good. International Journal of Behavioral Medicine, 12(2), 66–77.

- Seligman, M. E. P. (2011). Flourish: A Visionary New Understanding of Happiness and Well-Being. Free Press.

Chapter 20: Collective Transformation – Building Communities of Ease

When Amina moved into a new housing cooperative, she was struck by the difference from her previous neighborhood. Instead of isolation, there was connection. Neighbors shared meals, supported one another's projects, and celebrated milestones together. Decisions were made collaboratively, and even conflicts were approached with openness. Amina realized that transformation was not only individual; rather, it was collective, and communities could be built around ease, support, and shared growth. This experience taught her that the myth of life as hard was often reinforced by isolation, but when people come together with intention, they can create cultures of lightness, resilience, and care.

A Conversation

Karen: *We've talked a lot about individual transformation, but collective transformation is just as important, for communities shape the way we experience life.*

Mardoche: *Exactly. Research on social determinants of health shows that community conditions, such as safety, cohesion, and mutual support, are as important for well-being as individual choices.*

Karen: *Which means if we want to move beyond the myth of hardness, we need to build communities that model ease, spaces where people feel safe, valued, and connected.*

Mardoche: *And it doesn't take grand institutions; rather, it starts with small practices, such as shared meals, storytelling, and collaborative projects. These weave the fabric of belonging that makes transformation sustainable.*

Karen: *Transformation becomes not just an individual responsibility but a collective possibility.*

The Science of Collective Transformation

Public health research highlights the power of social connection for health and resilience. Studies show that strong social networks reduce mortality risk, improve mental health, and buffer against stress (Holt-Lunstad et al., 2010).

Community psychology emphasizes empowerment and participation. When individuals feel they have a voice and agency within their communities, both individual and collective outcomes improve (Zimmerman, 2000).

Sociological research also shows that cultures of mutual aid and collaboration increase resilience in the face of crises (Putnam, 2000). Communities built on trust and reciprocity thrive even under pressure, while fragmented ones struggle.

In short, transformation is amplified when it is shared. Collective ease creates conditions for individual flourishing, and individual transformation feeds back into stronger communities.

Tools for Reflection and Practice

1. **Community Mapping**: Identify the communities you belong to (neighborhood, workplace, spiritual, social). Reflect on where ease is present and where it is missing.

2. **Shared Rituals**: Create simple community rituals — shared meals, group reflections, or collective celebrations.

3. **Mutual Aid Practice**: Offer one act of support within your community this week. Notice how giving and receiving ease builds connection.

4. **Story Circles**: Gather a small group to share stories of resilience and joy. Storytelling fosters belonging and collective wisdom.

5. **Ease Audit for Communities**: With others, reflect on the question: 'How can we make our shared spaces feel lighter, safer, and more supportive?'

Closing Reflection

Collective transformation reminds us that we do not live in isolation. Amina's cooperative taught her that communities can be designed around ease, connection, and mutual growth. When we build cultures of support, individual transformation deepens and expands. The myth of hardness crumbles not only in the life of one person but in the shared life of many. Together, we can create communities where resilience is nurtured, belonging is celebrated, and joy becomes a collective norm.

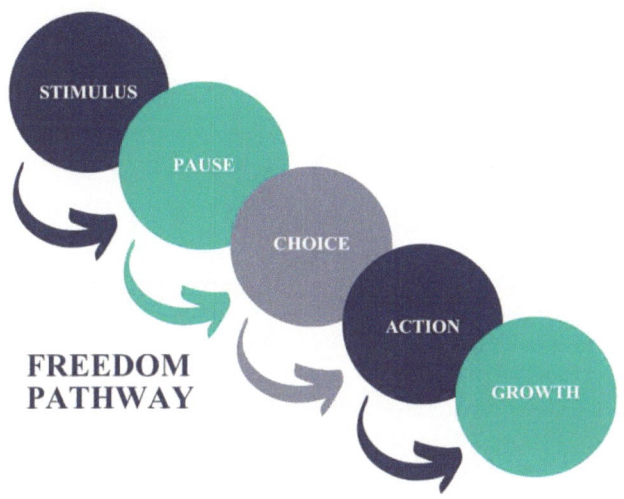

References

- Holt-Lunstad, J., Smith, T. B., & Layton, J. B. (2010). Social relationships and mortality risk: A meta-analytic review. PLoS Medicine, 7(7), e1000316.

- Putnam, R. D. (2000). Bowling Alone: The Collapse and Revival of American Community. Simon & Schuster.

- Zimmerman, M. A. (2000). Empowerment theory: Psychological, organizational, and community levels of analysis. In J. Rappaport & E. Seidman (Eds.), Handbook of Community Psychology (pp. 43–63). Springer.

Part IV: The Barriers to Ease

Chapter 21: Why We Cling to Hardness

Even as life offers moments of ease, many of us find ourselves returning to hardness, to struggle, overwork, and self-criticism. Sofia noticed this in herself. Whenever things felt light, she grew uneasy, as if she didn't deserve rest or joy. She would unconsciously create conflict at work, add unnecessary tasks to her schedule, or worry about problems that didn't exist. It was as if ease itself felt unsafe, and only later did she realize that she had internalized a belief: *'If it's not hard, it doesn't count.'* This chapter explores why so many of us cling to hardness, and not because we enjoy suffering, but because it has become familiar, protective, and even tied to our sense of identity.

A Conversation

Karen: *It's fascinating how people often resist ease, and when life feels good, they almost sabotage it.*

Mardoche: *Yes, and there are psychological reasons for this. For many, hardness equals worth. They've learned to equate struggle with virtue, and ease with laziness.*

Karen: *And for some, hardship becomes an identity. 'I am the one who survives difficulty.' Letting go of hardness can feel like losing part of themselves.*

Mardoche: *Not to mention defenses. Clinging to hardness can protect people from vulnerability. If I'm always struggling, I don't have to face the terror of ease or the openness of simply being.*

Karen: *Which means moving beyond hardness requires both compassion and courage. It's not about shaming people for clinging to struggle; rather, it's about helping them see new possibilities.*

The Science of Clinging to Hardness

Psychodynamic theory highlights the role of defenses in maintaining hardness. Patterns of overwork, self-criticism, or conflict can function as defenses against vulnerability (Freud, 1936).

Schema theory explains that many develop early maladaptive schemas such as unrelenting standards or defectiveness (Young et al., 2003). These schemas create the sense that only through struggle is one worthy of love or success.

Behavioral psychology suggests that struggle is often reinforced socially. Culturally, effort and exhaustion are praised, while rest and ease may be stigmatized as laziness (Hochschild, 1997).

Neuroscience adds that chronic stress can become habituated. The nervous system becomes accustomed to high cortisol states, so calm feels unfamiliar or even unsafe (McEwen, 2007).

Together, these perspectives explain why people cling to hardness and not because it's better, but because it feels safer, familiar, and validated.

Tools for Reflection and Practice

1. **Belief Inquiry**: Write down your beliefs about struggle and ease. Ask: *'Where did I learn this? Does it still serve me?'*
2. **Ease Exposure**: Intentionally allow moments of rest, joy, or play. Notice any discomfort. Reflect on what this reveals.
3. **Identity Reflection**: Consider how much of your identity is tied to surviving struggle. Ask: *'Who am I beyond hardship?'*
4. **Nervous System Reset**: Practice daily calming techniques (breath awareness, meditation, grounding). Help your body learn that ease is safe.
5. **Reframe Worth**: At the end of each day, write down one way you were valuable that did not involve struggle or suffering.

Closing Reflection

Clinging to hardness is not a failure; rather, it is a strategy, and one that once protected us but now holds us back. Sofia realized that her unease with joy was not proof that she didn't deserve it, but evidence of old conditioning. As she gently allowed herself more moments of lightness, her nervous system learned a new truth: life could be safe and meaningful without being hard. The path forward is not to reject struggle when it arises, but to stop worshiping it as the only path to worth. We can honor our resilience while also opening to the grace of ease.

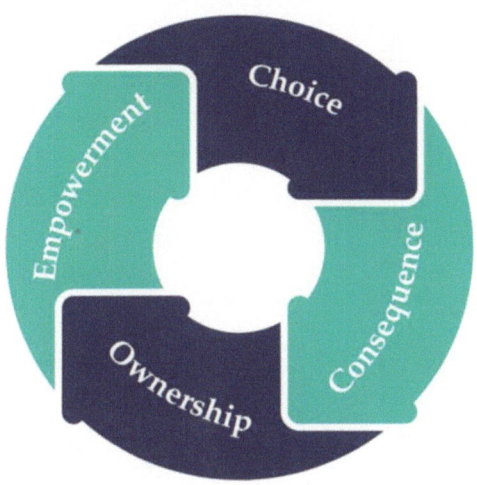

References

- Freud, A. (1936). The Ego and the Mechanisms of Defence. Hogarth Press.

- Hochschild, A. R. (1997). The Time Bind: When Work Becomes Home and Home Becomes Work. Metropolitan Books.

- McEwen, B. S. (2007). Physiology and neurobiology of stress and adaptation: Central role of the brain. Physiological Reviews, 87(3), 873–904.

- Young, J. E., Klosko, J. S., & Weishaar, M. E. (2003). Schema Therapy: A Practitioner's Guide. Guilford Press.

Chapter 22: The Hidden Comfort of Struggle

Marcus often complained about how hard his life was, about the long hours at work, the constant financial stress, and the tension in his relationships. However, when opportunities arose to ease his load, a promotion that offered more support, a partner's offer to share responsibility, he resisted. At first, he couldn't explain why, but with time, he realized something uncomfortable: struggle had become familiar, and gave him identity, routine, and even a sense of control. Without it, he felt lost, the struggle was hard, but it was also strangely comforting. This chapter explores why struggle, even when painful, can feel safe, and how we can move beyond its hidden comfort.

A Conversation

Karen: *It's remarkable how often people hold onto struggle even when relief is available.*

Mardoche: *Yes. On the surface, struggle feels miserable, but at a deeper level, it provides familiarity, identity, and sometimes even connection.*

Karen: *Right — think of people who bond over shared complaints. The struggle becomes a way of belonging.*

Mardoche: *And psychologically, struggle can mask vulnerability. If I stay focused on being overworked or overwhelmed, I don't have to face the scarier question: 'Who am I without this?'*

The Science of the Comfort in Struggle

Psychodynamic theory explains that repetition compulsion, the unconscious drive to repeat familiar struggles, often arises because what is familiar feels safer than what is unknown (Freud, 1920).

Schema theory shows that individuals with maladaptive schemas, such as unrelenting standards or deprivation, gravitate toward situations that confirm those schemas, reinforcing identity through struggle (Young et al., 2003).

Behavioral psychology adds that struggle can be socially rewarded. In many cultures, working long hours or enduring stress is praised, while choosing ease may be judged as laziness (Hochschild, 1997).

Neuroscience highlights habituation: the nervous system adapts to chronic stress. Over time, the body may perceive struggle as the baseline of safety, making calm feel foreign or even threatening (McEwen, 2007).

Together, these insights reveal why struggle can feel comforting — and why letting go of it requires intentional courage and practice.

Tools for Reflection and Practice
1. **Familiarity Check:** Ask yourself, 'What feels familiar about my current struggle? What would feel unfamiliar if I let it go?'
2. **Identity Expansion:** Write down how you describe yourself. Notice how much of your identity is tied to hardship. Imagine who you could be without those struggles.
3. **Joy Tolerance:** Practice allowing moments of joy or ease without sabotaging them. Notice any discomfort and reflect on its roots.
4. **Connection Shift:** Instead of bonding over shared complaints, create rituals of connection around joy, play, or creativity.
5. **Ease Experiments:** Intentionally choose one area of life where you allow ease. Reflect on how it feels and what fears arise.

Closing Reflection

The hidden comfort of struggle is one of life's paradoxes. What hurts can also feel safe, while what heals can feel threatening. Marcus discovered that his resistance to change wasn't laziness — it was fear of the unknown. As he slowly experimented with letting go of unnecessary struggle, he began to build a new comfort: ease, trust, and freedom. The comfort of struggle can keep us trapped, but the courage to step into ease opens the door to genuine growth.

References

- Freud, S. (1920). Beyond the Pleasure Principle. International Psycho-Analytical Press.

- Hochschild, A. R. (1997). The Time Bind: When Work Becomes Home and Home Becomes Work. Metropolitan Books.

- McEwen, B. S. (2007). Physiology and neurobiology of stress and adaptation: Central role of the brain. Physiological Reviews, 87(3), 873–904.

- Young, J. E., Klosko, J. S., & Weishaar, M. E. (2003). Schema Therapy: A Practitioner's Guide. Guilford Press.

Chapter 23: Defenses Against Lightness

When Alicia began therapy, she told her therapist that her greatest fear was not failure, but happiness. She confessed that whenever things felt good, she found ways to disrupt it, either by picking fights, doubting herself, or overloading her schedule. Lightness felt suspicious, and even dangerous. With time, she realized that her mind had built defenses against ease, happiness meant vulnerability, and vulnerability meant risk. This chapter explores the defenses we unconsciously construct against lightness, and how dismantling them opens the door to freedom.

A Conversation

Karen: *It's striking how often people defend against joy, as if it's something unsafe.*

Mardoche: *Yes. Freud described defenses as strategies to protect the ego from anxiety. For many, joy and lightness trigger anxiety because they feel temporary or undeserved.*

Karen: *Which means defenses like self-sabotage, perfectionism, or cynicism can all function as shields against ease.*

Mardoche: Exactly. *If I don't allow myself joy, I won't feel the pain of losing it. It's a misguided protection mechanism, but it feels safer than openness.*

Karen: *The paradox is that the very defenses that protect us also keep us from the life we long for.*

The Science of Defenses Against Lightness

Classical psychoanalysis identified defenses such as repression, denial, and projection as ways of managing painful emotions (Freud, 1936). Modern psychology expands this to include avoidance, perfectionism, and self-sabotage as strategies to avoid vulnerability (Cramer, 2000).

Schema theory adds that early maladaptive schemas, such as unworthiness or mistrust, often make joy feel unsafe, leading people to unconsciously block experiences of ease (Young et al., 2003).

Neuroscience reveals that chronic stress conditions the nervous system to expect threat. When safety or joy arises, the system may react with hypervigilance, as if danger is imminent (McEwen, 2007).

Together, these insights explain why defenses against lightness exist: they are attempts to protect against loss, disappointment, or vulnerability, but they also imprison us in struggle.

Tools for Reflection and Practice

1. **Defense Awareness**: Notice when you push away joy or ease. Ask: 'What defense am I using? Perfectionism? Cynicism? Self-sabotage?'

2. **Joy Tolerance Practice**: Each day, allow yourself one moment of joy without questioning or diminishing it. Notice any discomfort and breathe through it.

3. **Vulnerability Reflection**: Write about a time when joy felt unsafe. What belief was underneath that fear?

4. **Reframing Exercise**: When you catch yourself defending against lightness, pause and reframe: 'Lightness is not danger — it is nourishment.'

5. **Safe Lightness Ritual**: Create small rituals of ease (a walk, music, laughter) that you intentionally practice, teaching your nervous system that joy is safe.

Closing Reflection

Defenses against lightness are not signs of weakness; rather, they are signs of wounds and old strategies that once kept us safe. However, what once protected us can now hold us back. Alicia discovered that by slowly dismantling her defenses, she could allow herself to experience joy without fear. When we recognize and soften these defenses, we discover that lightness is not fragile; rather, it is resilient, steady, and deeply human, and to embrace it is to live fully, without apology.

Values-Actions-Outcomes Chart

References

- Cramer, P. (2000). Defense mechanisms in psychology today: Further processes for adaptation. American Psychologist, 55(6), 637–646.

- Freud, A. (1936). The Ego and the Mechanisms of Defence. Hogarth Press.

- McEwen, B. S. (2007). Physiology and neurobiology of stress and adaptation: Central role of the brain. Physiological Reviews, 87(3), 873–904.

- Young, J. E., Klosko, J. S., & Weishaar, M. E. (2003). Schema Therapy: A Practitioner's Guide. Guilford Press.

Chapter 24: Meeting Fear with Presence

Amira often described her fear as a shadow that followed her everywhere. She feared failure, rejection, loss, and even success. Her instinct was always to run, to distract herself, to over prepare, or to avoid risks altogether. one day, during a mindfulness retreat, she was invited to simply sit with her fear. Instead of analyzing or escaping it, she breathed into it, noticing the sensations in her body, and to her surprise, the fear softened; and while it didn't disappear, it no longer controlled her. Amira realized that fear wasn't the enemy; rather, it was a signal, and the way to respond was not with avoidance, but with presence.

A Conversation

Karen: *Fear often feels like a wall, but in reality, it's an invitation, and it's asking us to bring more presence, and not less.*

Mardoche: *Yes. When we avoid fear, it grows; and when we meet it with awareness, it transforms. Presence doesn't erase fear, but it changes our relationship to it.*

Karen: *And this is consistent with exposure therapy. Facing fears gradually, with safety and support, reduces their power.*

Mardoche: *And mindfulness research shows the same. Observing fear with curiosity reduces reactivity; and presence brings space, and space brings freedom.*

Karen: *Which means fear itself can become a teacher, if we're willing to sit with it.*

The Science of Meeting Fear

Neuroscience shows that fear activates the amygdala, the brain's threat detection system. When fear is avoided, the amygdala's response strengthens, reinforcing the cycle of fear (LeDoux, 1996).

Exposure therapy demonstrates that gradual, safe encounters with feared situations reduce fear over time through extinction learning (Craske et al., 2008).

Mindfulness research highlights that observing fear without judgment reduces activation of the default mode network and increases regulation of the prefrontal cortex, allowing calmer, more adaptive responses (Hölzel et al., 2011).

In short, presence interrupts fear's control. By staying with fear instead of fleeing, we retrain the brain to respond with awareness rather than reactivity.

Tools for Reflection and Practice

1. **Fear Mapping**: Write down your common fears. For each, note the sensations in your body when it arises.

2. **Breath Anchor**: When fear appears, take three slow breaths, grounding attention in your body instead of the fear story.

3. **Curiosity Practice**: Ask your fear, 'What are you trying to teach me?' Listen for the deeper message.

4. **Safe Exposure**: Choose one small fear and approach it gradually, with support if needed. Reflect on how your body responds.

5. **Presence Ritual**: Begin each day with five minutes of mindful sitting, practicing meeting whatever emotions arise with openness.

Closing Reflection

Fear is not proof of weakness; rather, it is a messenger, asking us to pay attention. Amira discovered that by meeting fear with presence, she could stop running and start listening. The shadow lost its power when she turned toward it with awareness; and when we meet fear with presence, we discover that fear itself is not the enemy, but avoidance is. In presence, fear becomes less of a wall and more of a doorway, guiding us deeper into courage, freedom, and authenticity.

Life Alignment Chart

References

- Craske, M. G., Kircanski, K., Zelikowsky, M., Mystkowski, J., Chowdhury, N., & Baker, A. (2008). Optimizing inhibitory learning during exposure therapy. Behaviour Research and Therapy, 46(1), 5–27.

- Hölzel, B. K., Lazar, S. W., Gard, T., Schuman-Olivier, Z., Vago, D. R., & Ott, U. (2011). How does mindfulness meditation work? Proposing mechanisms of action from a conceptual and neural perspective. Perspectives on Psychological Science, 6(6), 537–559.

- LeDoux, J. E. (1996). The Emotional Brain: The Mysterious Underpinnings of Emotional Life. Simon & Schuster.

Chapter 25: Beyond Trauma – Healing at All Four Layers

Leah had carried the weight of trauma for decades. Childhood neglect, betrayal, and violence had left deep imprints on her body and mind. She had tried therapy, medication, and self-help books, but nothing seemed to bring full relief. However, through a holistic program, she began to approach healing differently, and not only at the surface, but at every level. At the conscious layer, she built new habits of safety and self-care; while at the preconscious layer, she identified schemas of unworthiness that shaped her choices. At the unconscious layer, she uncovered repressed memories and patterns that silently guided her; while at the existential layer, she chose meaning and purpose beyond her trauma. For the first time, Leah felt not just recovery, but transformation. This chapter explores how healing trauma requires integration across all four layers.

A Conversation

Karen: *Trauma is often treated at only one level, and either through behavior change, cognitive reframing, or sometimes just symptom management.*

Mardoche: *Yes, but trauma lives in the body, in patterns, in the unconscious, and in meaning-making. Healing requires engaging all of those layers.*

Karen: *At the conscious level, safety and routine help stabilize daily life. But if we don't address schemas at the preconscious level, people stay stuck.*

Mardoche: *And without touching the unconscious — repressed memories, defenses, transference — trauma continues to leak into the present.*

Karen: *The existential layer is often overlooked. Choosing meaning beyond trauma is what turns survival into freedom.*

Mardoche: *Exactly. Healing at all four layers doesn't erase trauma, but it allows people to live beyond it.*

The Science of Trauma Healing Across Layers

Trauma research shows that adverse experiences alter both brain and body, including hyperactivation of the amygdala, dysregulation of cortisol, and fragmentation of memory (van der Kolk, 2014). Effective healing ought to therefore go beyond symptom reduction.

At the conscious level, cognitive-behavioral interventions build coping strategies and stabilize functioning (Foa et al., 2009). At the preconscious level, schema therapy identifies and reshapes maladaptive patterns rooted in early experience (Young et al., 2003).

At the unconscious level, psychodynamic and somatic approaches address repressed material, implicit memory, and bodily imprint (Levine, 1997). Dream work, free association, and relational repair open hidden dimensions of trauma.

At the existential layer, meaning-making frameworks like logotherapy emphasize that finding purpose transforms suffering into growth (Frankl, 1959).

Together, these approaches highlight that trauma cannot be healed in fragments. Whole healing requires layered integration.

Tools for Reflection and Practice

1. **Conscious – Safety Anchors**: Identify daily practices that create safety (rituals, routines, boundaries).

2. **Preconscious – Schema Journal**: Notice recurring themes (abandonment, unworthiness, mistrust). Reflect on their origins and challenge them.

3. **Unconscious – Dream Reflection**: Record dreams and slips of the tongue. Explore what hidden material may be surfacing.

4. **Existential – Meaning Statement**: Write a sentence beginning with 'My life stands for…' Revisit and revise it as you grow.

5. **Integration Practice**: Choose one healing action from each layer daily, weaving them into a holistic practice.

Closing Reflection

Trauma can fracture identity, but layered healing makes wholeness possible. Leah discovered that recovery was not about erasing her past, but about transforming her relationship to it. By working across the conscious, preconscious, unconscious, and existential layers, she found a freedom that no single approach had offered. Beyond trauma lies not only survival, but the possibility of a life lived with presence, meaning, and lightness. Healing at all four layers reminds us that we are more than what happened to us; rather, we are what we choose to become.

References

- Foa, E. B., Keane, T. M., Friedman, M. J., & Cohen, J. A. (2009). Effective Treatments for PTSD: Practice Guidelines from the International Society for Traumatic Stress Studies. Guilford Press.
- Frankl, V. E. (1959). Man's Search for Meaning. Beacon Press.
- Levine, P. A. (1997). Waking the Tiger: Healing Trauma. North Atlantic Books.
- van der Kolk, B. A. (2014). The Body Keeps the Score: Brain, Mind, and Body in the Healing of Trauma. Viking.
- Young, J. E., Klosko, J. S., & Weishaar, M. E. (2003). Schema Therapy: A Practitioner's Guide. Guilford Press.

Part V: The Existential Turn

Chapter 26: Choosing Freedom, Choosing Responsibility

Diego once believed freedom meant escape — from work, from family expectations, from responsibility. He chased freedom in travel, in spontaneity, and in breaking rules. Yet the more he ran, the less free he felt. His life became chaotic, disconnected, and empty. It was only when he began to see freedom not as avoidance but as alignment, choosing his responsibilities consciously, that everything shifted. By taking ownership of his choices, he felt a deeper, truer freedom. This chapter explores the paradox: that freedom and responsibility are not opposites, but partners.

A Conversation

Karen: *People often imagine freedom as the absence of responsibility, but in reality, freedom is about choosing our responsibilities.*

Mardoche: *Yes, Viktor Frankl said that freedom is only part of the story. The other half is responsibility; and without responsibility, freedom becomes emptiness.*

Karen: *And existential psychology tells us that true freedom is not doing whatever we want; rather, responding to life with awareness and values.*

Mardoche: *Which means freedom is not avoidance; rather, it's commitment, and it's choosing what and whom we will serve, consciously and with meaning.*

Karen: *That reframes freedom as not lightness without gravity, but as flight with direction.*

The Science of Freedom and Responsibility

Existential psychology emphasizes that freedom without responsibility leads to anxiety and despair (May, 1981; Frankl, 1959). Responsibility grounds freedom in meaning, transforming choice into purpose.

Self-determination theory (Deci & Ryan, 2000) shows that autonomy, which is the ability to choose, is a fundamental psychological need. However, autonomy flourishes most when aligned with intrinsic values, not external pressures.

Neuroscience explains how decision-making engages brain regions linked to both reward and executive control. Freedom without responsibility activates only short-term pleasure centers, while responsible choices engage networks associated with long-term fulfillment (Miller & Cuttler, 2003).

Together, these perspectives highlight that freedom is not just release from constraints; rather, it is the active choice of responsibility aligned with meaning.

Tools for Reflection and Practice

1. **Freedom Inventory**: List the areas of your life where you feel free but unanchored. Ask: *'What responsibility could give this freedom direction?'*

2. **Responsibility Reframe**: Choose one obligation you resent. Reframe it as a chosen responsibility — why does it matter to you?

3. **Values Alignment**: Write down your top three values. Reflect: 'How can I take responsibility today that reflects these values?'

4. **Choice Pause**: Before making a decision, pause and ask: 'Am I choosing avoidance, or am I choosing aligned responsibility?'

5. **Existential Compass**: Create a statement that links your freedom and responsibility: *'I am free to… and I choose to…'* Repeat it daily.

Closing Reflection

Diego discovered that freedom without responsibility is not liberation but drift. It was only when he chose responsibility for his relationships, his work, and his purpose, that he felt truly free. Freedom and responsibility are not enemies. They are dance partners, each giving the other meaning. To choose freedom without responsibility is to float aimlessly; and to choose responsibility without freedom is to suffocate. However, when we choose both, we find the paradoxical gift: a life of lightness, direction, and meaning.

DAILY INTEGRATION CHECKLIST

- [ ] Conscious (Habits, Routines)
- [ ] Preconscious (Beliefs, Schemas)
- [ ] Unconscious (Insights, Shadow)
- [ ] Existential (Meaning, Purpose)

References

- Deci, E. L., & Ryan, R. M. (2000). Self-determination theory and the facilitation of intrinsic motivation, social development, and well-being. American Psychologist, 55(1), 68–78.
- Frankl, V. E. (1959). Man's Search for Meaning. Beacon Press.
- May, R. (1981). Freedom and Destiny. W.W. Norton & Company.
- Miller, E. K., & Cuttler, A. (2003). Cognitive control and the prefrontal cortex: The role of reward in decision-making. Nature Neuroscience, 6(2), 215–219.

Chapter 27: The Compass of Values

When Farah felt lost in her career, she tried making pro-and-con lists, seeking advice, even flipping a coin. But nothing brought clarity. Then her mentor asked a different question: 'What do you value most?' Farah paused. She had never really thought of decisions that way. As she reflected, she realized her deepest values were growth, contribution, and authenticity. Suddenly, the path became clearer, and she would pursue the opportunity that aligned most with these values, even if it wasn't the most lucrative. In that moment, Farah discovered that values are not abstract ideals; rather, they are a compass, guiding us toward meaning, direction, and integrity.

A Conversation

Karen: *When people feel lost, they often look outside for answers. However, clarity usually comes from within and from values.*

Mardoche: *Yes, values act like a compass. They don't tell us exactly what to do, but they point us in the right direction.*

Karen: *And this is central to Acceptance and Commitment Therapy. ACT teaches that when we live in alignment with values, even painful experiences become meaningful.*

Mardoche: *Exactly. Struggle feels less like suffering when it serves a higher purpose. Further, values give direction to freedom and responsibility.*

Karen: *Which means that living by values is not about perfection, but about orientation, and about coming back to the compass again and again.*

The Science of Values as Compass

Acceptance and Commitment Therapy (ACT) emphasizes values as central to psychological flexibility. Living in alignment with values reduces avoidance and increases resilience (Hayes et al., 1999).

Research on self-determination theory shows that when behaviors are guided by intrinsic values, rather than external pressures, they foster greater well-being, motivation, and life satisfaction (Deci & Ryan, 2000).

Neuroscience supports that decisions aligned with personal values activate reward pathways in the brain, reinforcing positive emotion and meaning (Kang et al., 2017).

In short, values function as an inner compass, providing direction even when circumstances are uncertain.

Tools for Reflection and Practice

1. **Values Clarification**: Write down your top five values. Ask yourself: *'Which of these do I actually live by daily? Which do I neglect?'*

2. **Compass Check**: Before making a decision, pause and ask: *'Which option aligns most with my values?'*

3. **Daily Alignment**: Choose one value each morning. Ask: *'How will I live this value today?'*

4. **Conflict Reflection**: Think of a recent conflict. How did your values shape your perspective? How might recognizing the other person's values bring understanding?

5. **Existential Statement**: Complete the sentence: *'No matter what happens, I want my life to stand for...'* Use this as your north star.

Closing Reflection

Farah discovered that her compass had been within her all along. Values don't eliminate uncertainty, but they make the path clearer and more meaningful. When we live by values, we no longer measure life only in terms of ease or struggle; rather, we measure it by integrity, alignment, and purpose. Furthermore, the compass of values does not prevent storms, but it ensures that we move in the direction of our deepest truths; and that is where lightness and meaning are found.

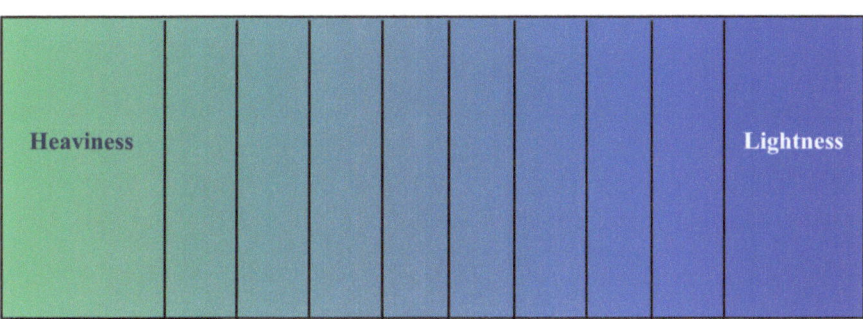

References

- Deci, E. L., & Ryan, R. M. (2000). Self-determination theory and the facilitation of intrinsic motivation, social development, and well-being. American Psychologist, 55(1), 68–78.

- Hayes, S. C., Strosahl, K., & Wilson, K. G. (1999). Acceptance and Commitment Therapy: An Experiential Approach to Behavior Change. Guilford Press.

- Kang, Y., Gray, J. R., & Dovidio, J. F. (2017). The neuroscience of values and value-based decision-making. Journal of Economic Psychology, 62, 137–150.

Chapter 28: The Golden Rule Reimagined

As a child, Amir was taught the Golden Rule: *'Do unto others as you would have them do unto you.'* He tried to live by it, but as he grew older, he realized it wasn't always simple. He valued honesty, so he was blunt with friends, but sometimes it hurt them. He loved surprises, so he planned them for others, but not everyone enjoyed them. One day, his mentor offered a new perspective: *'The Golden Rule isn't about giving others what **you** want. It's about recognizing their values, their needs, and treating them with dignity.'* Amir realized the Golden Rule could be reimagined, and not as a one-size-fits-all principle, but as a guide to empathy, respect, and relational lightness.

A Conversation

Karen: *The Golden Rule has shaped ethics for centuries, but people often misunderstand it.*

Mardoche: *Yes, if we only do to others what we want, we risk imposing our own preferences. Real empathy means asking, 'What matters to them?'*

Karen: *Exactly. This is why some suggest the **'Platinum Rule,'** which is to do unto others as they would want done to them.*

Mardoche: *Which brings us back to presence. Lightness in relationships comes when we listen deeply, treat others with dignity, and honor their uniqueness.*

Karen: *So, reimagining the Golden Rule is less about rigid morality and more about living compassion as a daily practice.*

The Science of Empathy and Reciprocity

Moral psychology shows that fairness and reciprocity are universal human values, appearing in cultures across the world (Haidt, 2001). The Golden Rule reflects this innate drive for justice and empathy.

Research on empathy demonstrates that perspective-taking, which is imagining the world from another's viewpoint, increases compassion, reduces bias, and strengthens relationships (Batson, 2011).

Neuroscience reveals that empathy activates mirror neurons and brain regions involved in social connection, reinforcing bonds and cooperative behavior (Decety & Jackson, 2004).

In short, reimagining the Golden Rule means practicing empathy not as projection but as presence, meeting others where they are, while still rooted in our own integrity.

Tools for Reflection and Practice

1. **Empathy Pause**: In conversations, pause and ask, *'What does this person value right now?'* before responding.

2. **Platinum Practice**: Experiment with the Platinum Rule — treat others as **they** would like to be treated. Reflect on how this shifts your relationships.

3. **Value Alignment**: Ask friends, family, or colleagues directly: *'What feels supportive to you?'* Notice how their answers may differ from your own.

4. **Compassion Ritual**: Each morning, choose one act of kindness you will extend — not based on your preference, but on another's need.

5. **Integrity Check**: While honoring others, ask: *'Am I still aligned with my own values?'* True empathy balances self and other.

Closing Reflection

Amir discovered that the Golden Rule was not about imposing his way of being on others, but about honoring their uniqueness with compassion. Reimagining the Golden Rule invites us to live with deeper empathy, and balancing our integrity with respect for others' values. This shift transforms relationships from obligation into presence, and from hardness into lightness. The rule remains golden, not because it is rigid, but because it shines brighter when reimagined through empathy and love.

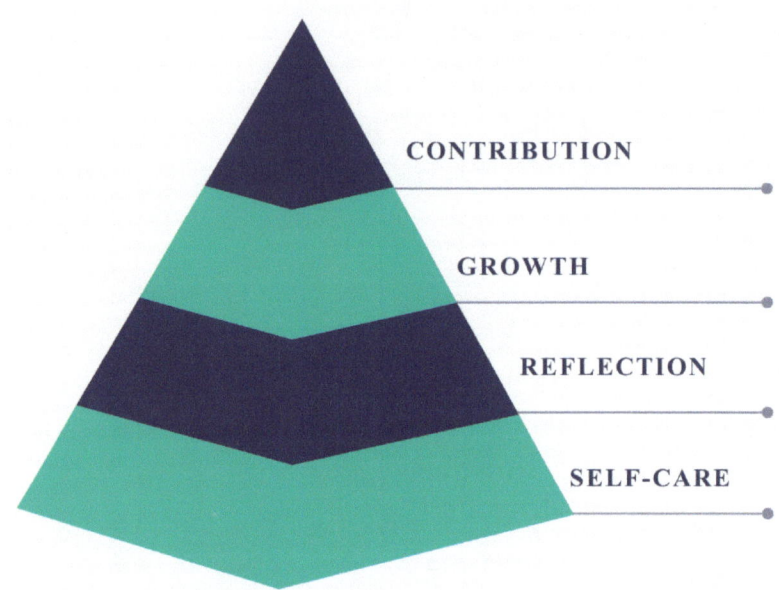

References

- Batson, C. D. (2011). Altruism in Humans. Oxford University Press.

- Decety, J., & Jackson, P. L. (2004). The functional architecture of human empathy. Behavioral and Cognitive Neuroscience Reviews, 3(2), 71–100.

- Haidt, J. (2001). The emotional dog and its rational tail: A social intuitionist approach to moral judgment. Psychological Review, 108(4), 814–834.

Chapter 29: The Existential Leap – Saying Yes to Life

When Naomi faced a major health crisis, she found herself asking the deepest questions: *'Why go on? What is the point?'* For months she felt paralyzed, caught between despair and the longing for meaning. One morning, she sat watching the sunrise, and a thought emerged, and not as logic, but as a quiet certainty: *'I choose to say yes.'* Yes, to the uncertainty, yes to the pain, yes to the possibility of joy. This was her existential leap, and not denying suffering, but embracing life as it is, with freedom and courage. This chapter explores what it means to take that leap: to affirm life even when it is uncertain, imperfect, and unpredictable.

A Conversation

Karen: *Existential thinkers often speak of the leap — that moment when we move from doubt to affirmation.*

Mardoche: *Yes, Kierkegaard spoke of the 'leap of faith,' and Nietzsche described saying 'yes' to life even with all its suffering.*

Karen: *And Frankl reminded us that even in suffering, life holds meaning — and it is our task to choose it.*

Mardoche: *The leap is not about certainty; rather, it's about commitment; and t's about choosing to engage with life fully, without waiting for guarantees.*

Karen: *Which means saying yes is less about circumstances and more about orientation — a stance of courage and presence.*

The Science of Saying Yes to Life

Existential psychology emphasizes that embracing freedom and responsibility is essential to living authentically (May, 1981; Frankl, 1959). Choosing life despite uncertainty fosters resilience and meaning.

Positive psychology research shows that life affirmation, which is to be consciously focusing on meaning, gratitude, and purpose, is linked to greater well-being, even in the face of adversity (Seligman, 2011).

Neuroscience adds that practices like gratitude and meaning-making activate brain networks associated with positive emotion and resilience, supporting psychological growth (Fox et al., 2015).

Together, these perspectives suggest that the existential leap is not denial of hardship, but the embrace of life as a whole, and a choice that transforms despair into possibility.

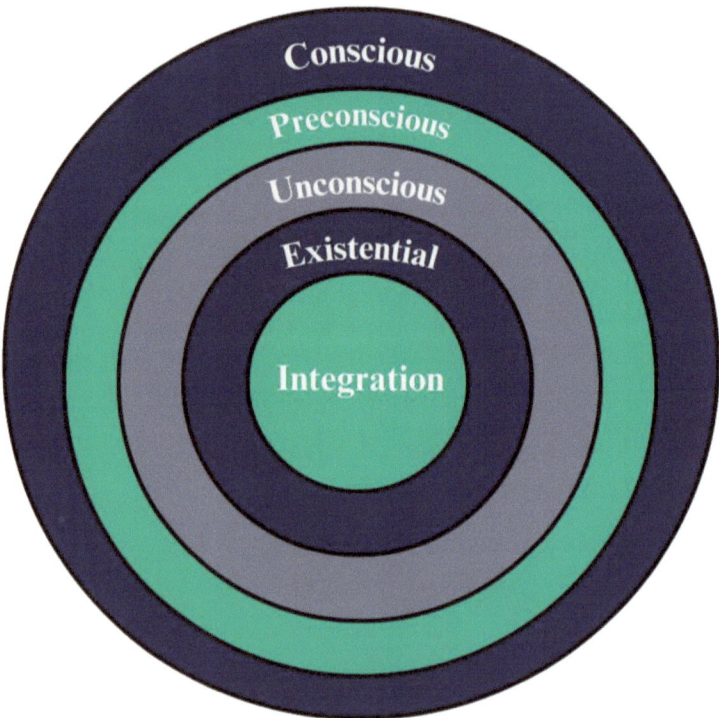

Tools for Reflection and Practice

1. **Daily Yes Practice**: Each morning, whisper to yourself, 'I say yes to life today,' and notice how it shapes your choices.
2. **Meaning Statement**: Write a short sentence about why you choose life — even amidst uncertainty. Place it somewhere visible.
3. **Gratitude Anchor**: Each evening, write down one moment when you felt glad to be alive.
4. **Existential Journal**: Reflect on the question: 'What am I willing to say yes to, even without guarantees?'
5. **Courage Ritual**: When faced with fear, take one small action that embodies your 'yes' — a phone call, a step forward, a breath of presence.

Closing Reflection

Naomi discovered that saying yes to life did not erase her pain or uncertainty; rather, it gave her a way forward, and a compass of courage and meaning. The existential leap is not about waiting for life to prove itself worthy; rather, it is about choosing to affirm life in every moment, even amidst doubt. When we say yes, we stop postponing living, we discover that life, with all its contradictions, is already enough, and that our yes transforms it into a gift.

References

- Frankl, V. E. (1959). Man's Search for Meaning. Beacon Press.
- Fox, K. C. R., Nijeboer, S., Dixon, M. L., Floman, J. L., Ellamil, M., Rumak, S. P.,& Christoff, K. (2015). Is meditation associated with altered brain structure? A systematic review and meta-analysis of morphometric neuroimaging in meditation practitioners. Neuroscience & Biobehavioral Reviews, 43, 48–73.
- May, R. (1981). Freedom and Destiny. W.W. Norton & Company.
- Seligman, M. E. P. (2011). Flourish: A Visionary New Understanding of Happiness and Well-being. Free Press.

Chapter 30: Life as Grace

On her 80th birthday, Clara stood before her family and friends, tears in her eyes. She spoke not of her achievements, nor of her struggles, but of grace. *'Life has been many things,'* she said, *'but what I see now is that it has always been a gift; and not because it was easy; rather, because it was fair, because it was given, and I chose to receive it.'* Clara's words reflected a truth that transcends hardship and ease: life itself, in all its contradictions, is grace. This chapter closes the journey by exploring what it means to live in grace, and not as perfection or avoidance of struggle, but as a deep acceptance of life as gift, and of ourselves as participants in that gift.

A Conversation

Karen: *We've talked about lightness, integration, and saying yes to life. Grace feels like the culmination of all of these.*

Mardoche: *Yes, grace is not something we earn; rather, t's something we recognize; and it's seeing life as gift, and not as a transaction.*

Karen: *And when we live in grace, struggle loses its centrality; and we stop defining ourselves by how hard life is.*

Mardoche: *Exactly. Grace reframes both hardship and ease. It reminds us that even in suffering, there can be beauty; and even in joy, there can be humility.*

Karen: *So, grace is not about denying reality, but about embracing it fully, with presence, gratitude, and compassion.*

The Science of Grace and Gratitude

Positive psychology research demonstrates that gratitude, which is the recognition of life as gift, is strongly correlated with well-being, resilience, and relational health (Emmons & McCullough, 2003).

Neuroscience shows that gratitude practices activate brain regions associated with reward, empathy, and moral cognition, shifting perspective from scarcity to abundance (Zahn et al., 2009).

Spiritual and existential psychology highlight that grace involves acceptance and humility, cultivating a sense of connection beyond the self (Pargament, 2007).

Together, these insights suggest that grace is not only a spiritual concept; rather, a psychological orientation, and a way of perceiving life that brings peace, meaning, and integration.

Tools for Reflection and Practice

1. **Daily Grace Reflection**: Each evening, write down one moment when life felt like a gift, however small.

2. **Graceful Reframe**: When facing hardship, ask: 'Where might grace still be present in this experience?'

3. **Gratitude Practice**: Begin or end your day by listing three things you are grateful for, no matter how ordinary.

4. **Offering Grace**: Extend compassion to someone today — not because they earned it, but because grace is freely given.

5. **Existential Pause**: Sit quietly for five minutes, simply noticing your breath and your being. Reflect: 'What does it mean that life itself is a gift?'

Closing Reflection

Clara's words remind us that the final step of transformation is neither effort, nor understanding, but grace. To live as grace is to live in deep recognition: life does not have to be hard, nor does it have to be easy. It simply is, and in its being, it is gift. When we see life this way, we discover a lightness that no struggle can erase. Grace does not eliminate suffering, but it infuses it with meaning. Grace does not guarantee ease, but it opens us to joy. To live in grace is to live free, whole, and at peace; and not because life is perfect, but because life is enough.

References

- Emmons, R. A., & McCullough, M. E. (2003). Counting blessings versus burdens: An experimental investigation of gratitude and subjective well-being in daily life. Journal of Personality and Social Psychology, 84(2), 377–389.
- Pargament, K. I. (2007). Spiritually Integrated Psychotherapy: Understanding and Addressing the Sacred. Guilford Press.
- Zahn, R., Garrido, G., Moll, J., & Grafman, J. (2009). Individual differences in posterior cortical volume correlate with proneness to pride and gratitude. Social Cognitive and Affective Neuroscience, 4(4), 317–326.

Conclusion

We began with a question: Does life have to be hard?

Through these chapters, we have explored another possibility, that while struggle is part of the human condition, it does not have to define the human experience. Life can be lived differently, growth can emerge not only from hardship, and also from presence, joy, connection, and grace.

We walked through the ***Four Layers of Transformation***:
- At the conscious layer, you discovered the power of habits, routines, and structure.
- At the preconscious layer, you uncovered the beliefs and patterns shaping your choices.
- At the unconscious layer, you touched the hidden material that influences you from the depths.
- At the existential layer, you chose meaning, purpose, and freedom.

Together, these layers offer a path of integration. They remind us that transformation is not only possible but sustainable when we work across all levels of our being.

This book is not the end of the process, but the beginning of practice, for every breath, every choice, every relationship becomes a place where lightness can be cultivated. You now hold the tools to shift from hardness to ease, from effort to flow, and from fragmentation to wholeness.

The conclusion is not a closing statement but an opening door. It is an invitation to live as though life is not defined by struggle; rather, illuminated by grace. May you carry this truth with you: life does not have to be hard. It can be lived in freedom, with lightness, and with love.

Epilogue

Life Is Not Hard

As we reach the final page, we return to the truth that carried us here: Life is not hard.

Yes, life is not linear. It brings joys and sorrows, beginnings and endings. However, hardness, the sense that we must always fight, endure, and struggle in order to be worthy, is a story we were taught, not a reality we ought to live. This book has been about unlearning that story.

Through the ***Four Layers of Transformation*** — conscious, preconscious, unconscious, and existential — we have explored how change truly happens. We have seen that habits, beliefs, hidden patterns, and meaning all play a role in shaping how we experience life. When we tend to each of these layers, we no longer relate to life as a battle; rather, we begin to live as though ease, joy, and grace are possible, for they are.

The invitation of this book is not to deny challenges; rather, it is to see them differently. It is to remember that even in the midst of difficulty, life is not hard; rather life simply is, and within its unfolding, there is always lightness to be found.

As you step away from these pages, may you carry this truth into your daily life. May you pause when struggle feels overwhelming and remind yourself: hardness is not a requirement; rather, growth can come through presence, healing can come through love, and transformation can come through grace.

Life is not hard; rather, it is whole, it is enough, and it is yours to live with freedom, with purpose, and with lightness.

Invitation to the Reader

As you close this book, we want to leave you with an invitation.

First, pause. Reflect on what resonated most with you. Was it a story? A scientific insight? A practice that you are ready to try? Write it down. Commit to carrying it with you into the days ahead. Transformation is not in what we know, but in what we practice.

Second, choose one action. It does not need to be grand. It might be a breath before reacting, a moment of kindness, or the choice to see a challenge through the lens of lightness rather than hardness. Let this book become not only something you have read, but something you live.

Third, share. We do not transform alone. We grow in community, through connection, reflection, and encouragement. Share what you are learning with a friend, a colleague, or a loved one. Your words may be the invitation they need to discover that life, too, does not have to be hard.

Finally, if this book has spoken to you, we humbly ask that you leave a review. Reviews help this message reach others who are searching for a new way of living. Your reflection, just a few sentences of what the book meant to you, could help light the path for someone else.

This is more than a book. It is a movement, and a shift from hardness to lightness, from struggle to grace. Thank you for being part of it.

With gratitude,

Mardoche Sidor, MD
Karen Dubin, PhD, LCSW

Final Acknowledgments

As we bring this book to a close, our hearts are filled with gratitude.

To our readers, thank you. By picking up this book, by engaging with its questions and practices, you have joined us in reimagining what it means to live. Your willingness to explore a new way of being is what gives this work life beyond the page.

To our colleagues, students, and community at the SWEET Institute, your energy, curiosity, and dedication continue to inspire us. You remind us that knowledge becomes transformation only when it is shared, practiced, and lived together.

To our teams at Urban Pathways and beyond, thank you for your unwavering commitment to those who too often live under the weight of hardship. Your work is proof that presence, compassion, and dignity are stronger than struggle.

To our families, your love, patience, and encouragement sustained us throughout this journey. Every page is touched by your presence.

Finally, to the countless voices, past, present, and future, who whisper the truth that inspired this book: life is not hard. Thank you for reminding us, again and again, of what really matters.

With abiding gratitude and hope,

Mardoche Sidor, MD
Karen Dubin, PhD, LCSW

Reader Integration Toolkit

From Message to Practice

This toolkit is designed to help you move from reading to living. Each exercise, chart, and prompt is a bridge from insight to integration. Use them at your own pace, and return to them often, for the more you practice, the more natural lightness becomes.

1. Conscious Layer – Habits & Daily Practices

   a. **Morning Ritual Checklist**: Breath awareness (2 min), gratitude statement, daily intention.
   b. **Evening Reflection**: One moment of ease, one thing learned, one step forward.
   c. **Lifestyle Anchor Chart**: Sleep, nutrition, movement, and stress-care — track daily for 14 days.

2. Preconscious Layer – Beliefs & Patterns

   a. **Core Belief Mapping**: Write one repeating thought you notice. Ask: Where did this begin? Does it serve me today?
   b. **Schema Reframe Exercise**: Identify a limiting story → Rewrite it as an empowering statement.
   c. **Dialogue with Self**: Spend 5 minutes journaling in "question & answer" style with your inner voice.

3. Unconscious Layer – Hidden Material

   a. **Dream Journal Template**: Record dreams upon waking; underline repeating themes.
   b. **Free Association Practice**: Choose a word (e.g., "ease"), write continuously for 5 minutes without editing.
   c. **Defense Awareness Tracker**: Notice one moment of avoidance, rationalization, or projection. Pause and write what you were protecting.

4. Existential Layer – Meaning & Freedom

   a. **Values Clarification Worksheet**: List 10 values, circle 3 most important, design one action for each.
   b. **Golden Rule Reflection**: Each week, ask: Did I treat others as I wish to be treated? Write examples.
   c. **Purpose Statement**: Draft a 1–2 sentence vision of the life you want to live. Place it somewhere visible.

5. Integration Practice – Weekly Alignment

   a. **Weekly Review:**
      i. What worked this week?
      ii. What felt heavy?
      iii. Where did I practice ease?
      iv. What will I try next week?
   b. **Accountability Partner Prompt**: Share one intention with someone you trust. Check in weekly.

6. Reflection & Growth

   a. **Lightness Scale (1–10):** Each evening, rate the day on how light or heavy it felt. Track trends over time.
   b. **Commitment Contract**: Write, sign, and date: I commit to practicing lightness in my daily life, one choice at a time.

This toolkit is not about perfection. It is about practice. Each small act of awareness, each moment of ease, each choice of presence is a step into the truth of this book: life is not hard.

Appendix

Tools, Exercises, Charts, and Frameworks

This appendix gathers the key tools from the book into one place. Use it as a quick reference or as a companion to deepen your practice.

1. Tools for the Conscious Layer

Morning Ritual Checklist:

- ☐ Breath awareness (2 minutes)
- ☐ Gratitude statement
- ☐ Daily intention

Evening Reflection Prompts:

- ☐ One moment of ease
- ☐ One thing learned
- ☐ One step forward

Lifestyle Anchor Chart – 14 Days

Day	Sleep (hrs)	Nutrition (✓/✗)	Movement (mins)	Stress-Care (✓/✗)
1				
2				
3				
4				
5				
6				
7				
8				
9				
10				
11				
12				
13				
14				

2. Tools for the Preconscious Layer

Core Belief Mapping Table:

Repeating Thought	Origin	Does it serve me today?

Schema Reframe Exercise:

Limiting Story	Empowering Statement

Dialogue with Self:

(Use the space below for journaling in Q&A style.)

3. Tools for the Unconscious Layer

Dream Journal Template:

Date	Dream Content	Themes/Patterns

Free Association Practice:

Choose a word and write continuously for 5 minutes without editing.

_____
_____
_____
_____
_____
_____
_____
_____
_____
_____
_____
_____
_____
_____

Defense Awareness Tracker:

Situation	Defense Noticed	What Was I Protecting?

4. Tools for the Existential Layer

Values Clarification Worksheet:

Value	Importance (1–10)	One Action Step

Golden Rule Reflection:

Did I treat others as I wish to be treated? Write examples below:

Purpose Statement:

Draft a 1–2 sentence vision of the life you want to live.

5. Integration Charts & Frameworks

Weekly Integration Review:

Question	Your Reflection
What worked this week?	
What felt heavy?	
Where did I practice ease?	
What will I try next week?	

Lightness Scale (1–10):

Date	Lightness (1–10)	Notes

Commitment Contract:

I commit to practicing lightness in my daily life, one choice at a time.

Signed: _____

Date: _____

6. The Four Layers of Transformation Framework

1. Conscious Layer – Habits, routines, accountability, discipline
2. Preconscious Layer – Core beliefs, schemas, attachment patterns
3. Unconscious Layer – Repressed material, dreams, defenses, free associations
4. Existential Layer – Meaning, freedom, purpose, ethics, integration

This framework is the backbone of the book, guiding readers from surface-level change to deep integration.

Recommended Reading

The following books have shaped the ideas in *Life Is Not Hard* and can serve as companions on your journey of transformation:

Psychology, Growth, and Healing

- Frankl, V. E. (1959). *Man's Search for Meaning*. Beacon Press.
- Seligman, M. E. P. (2011). Flourish: A Visionary New Understanding of Happiness and Well-being. Atria Books.
- Beck, J. S. (2021). *Cognitive Behavior Therapy: Basics and Beyond* (3rd ed.). Guilford Press.
- Young, J. E., Klosko, J. S., & Weishaar, M. E. (2003). *Schema Therapy: A Practitioner's Guide*. Guilford Press.

Mindfulness and Presence

- Kabat-Zinn, J. (1994). Wherever You Go, There You Are: Mindfulness Meditation in Everyday Life. Hyperion.
- Nhat Hanh, T. (1999). The Miracle of Mindfulness: An Introduction to the Practice of Meditation. Beacon Press.
- Tolle, E. (2004). The Power of Now: A Guide to Spiritual Enlightenment. New World Library.

Neuroscience and Human Behavior

- Siegel, D. J. (2012). The Developing Mind: How Relationships and the Brain Interact to Shape Who We Are (2nd ed.). Guilford Press.
- LeDoux, J. (2015). Anxious: Using the Brain to Understand and Treat Fear and Anxiety. Viking.
- Davidson, R. J., & Begley, S. (2012). *The Emotional Life of Your Brain*. Plume.

Existential and Philosophical Perspectives

- Yalom, I. D. (1980). *Existential Psychotherapy*. Basic Books.

- May, R. (1983). *The Discovery of Being*. W. W. Norton & Company.
- de Mello, A. (1992). Awareness: The Perils and Opportunities of Reality. Image Books.

Practical Guides for Living Lightly

- Brown, B. (2010). *The Gifts of Imperfection*. Hazelden Publishing.
- Neff, K. (2011). Self-Compassion: The Proven Power of Being Kind to Yourself. William Morrow.
- Clear, J. (2018). Atomic Habits: An Easy & Proven Way to Build Good Habits & Break Bad Ones. Avery.

These readings are not required, but they offer perspectives, practices, and insights that expand on the themes of this book — resilience, mindfulness, transformation, and meaning.

More from SWEET Institute Publishing

SWEET Institute Publishing is dedicated to producing transformational books for a transformational world. Each title is designed to bridge science and practice, reflection and action, so that readers not only understand new ideas but live them.

Recently Published Titles
- Before Anything Else, Validate
- The Courage to Care: Stories of Healing, Hope, and the Power of Social Work
- Rewriting the Script: Healing Inner Dialogue and Ending Internalized Oppression Forthcoming Releases
- The Still Point
- The Simplicity Principle
- The Kindness Imperative: How Power Becomes Purpose, and Why True Greatness Begins with Grace
- How Life Works
- Breaking the Pattern: Understanding and Healing Repetition Compulsion
- Freeing Fear: A Journey Through the Mind – Conscious, Preconscious, and Unconscious
- The Anchor Blueprint: Redefining Care for the Forgotten, the Misunderstood, and the High Acuity

We invite you to explore these works as companions on your journey. Each book is a pathway toward presence, healing, and transformation, for yourself, your relationships, and the communities you serve.

About the Authors

Mardoche Sidor, MD

Dr. Mardoche Sidor is a Harvard- and Columbia-trained quadruple board-certified psychiatrist (General Psychiatry, Child and Adolescent Psychiatry, Addiction Psychiatry, and Forensic Psychiatry). He has also trained in Public/Community Psychiatry and Geriatric Psychiatry. Dr. Sidor served as Assistant Clinical Professor of Psychiatry at Columbia University for eight years and currently serves as the Medical Director of Urban Pathways, a leading supportive housing and service organization in New York City.

He is the founder of the SWEET Institute (Supporting Wellbeing through Empowerment, Education, and Training), where he leads transformative learning experiences for clinicians worldwide. His mission is to bridge the gap between knowledge and implementation, blending science, philosophy, and practical tools for real-world transformation.

Karen Dubin, PhD, LCSW

Dr. Karen Dubin is a clinical social worker, researcher, and educator with a PhD in Social Work and decades of experience supporting individuals, families, and communities. She is widely respected for her contributions to mental health education, supervision, and program development.

As the co-founder of the SWEET Institute, Dr. Dubin has co-created innovative programs, facilitated healing circles, and co-authored multiple works aimed at transforming clinical practice. Her voice weaves together academic rigor and deep compassion, ensuring that learning is not only intellectual but also experiential and lasting.

SWEET Institute Publishing

This book is published under SWEET Institute Publishing: Transformational Books for a Transformational World. Through its publications, SWEET brings forward the integration of science, presence, and practice, empowering clinicians, leaders, and everyday readers to step into lives of purpose, freedom, and lightness.

Together, Dr. Sidor and Dr. Dubin have co-authored numerous books, programs, and frameworks to advance healing, growth, and transformation, for individuals, communities, and the field of mental health at large.

www.ingramcontent.com/pod-product-compliance
Lightning Source LLC
Chambersburg PA
CBHW041621220426
43662CB00001B/7